New York City: 1900-1923
A Collection of Poetry

New York City: 1900-1923
A Collection of Poetry

Edited with an introduction by

Hannah Watt

WHITLOCK PUBLISHING
ALFRED, N.Y.

First Whitlock Publishing Edition 2019

Whitlock Publishing
www.whitlockpublishing.com

ISBN 13: 978-1-943115-36-5

This book was set in Adobe Garamond Pro on 50# acid-free paper that meets ANSI standards for archival quality.

Table of Contents

Acknowledgements

I would like to thank Dr. Allen Grove for making the publishing of this anthology possible and for his help and guidance along the way.

I would also like to thank my parents, Richard and Tara, and my brother, Devin, for their endless love and support.

Introduction

In his 1908 poem "New Buildings," Charles Hanson Towne comments on the transformation of New York City: "The turrets leap higher and higher / And the little old homes go down." He specifically touches on rapid industrialization and new construction while other poets, such as Amy Lowell, focus on new modes of transportation in New York. Some writers criticized the city's growth with its pollution and unfit working conditions, while others admired its beautiful new lights and buildings. Immigration also changed the city; it added new voices to poetry as the population more than double from 1900 until 1923. A new literary movement, The Harlem Renaissance, did the same. African Americans in Harlem expressed themselves and found their own distinctive voices during the early twentieth century. Imagism also emerged during this period as its most famous practitioner, Ezra Pound, explored the idea that an image "presents an intellectual and emotional complex in an instant of time."

Many early twentieth-century poets wrote about the new buildings that were changing the Manhattan skyline. Two modern structures during this time are the

Metropolitan Tower and the Woolworth Building. In his poem "City Roofs (From the Metropolitan Tower)," Charles Hanson Towne's narrator is high up in the Metropolitan Life Tower reflecting on what the roof-tops below him are covering. He also contemplates the lack of privacy homeless people have and how this leads to their innocence. The Metropolitan Life Insurance Tower was completed in 1909 at the request of John Rogers Hegeman to expand his company's headquarters. It is a campanile-style tower that stands at 5 Madison Avenue between East 23rd and East 24th Streets. It is 700 feet tall, making it the world's tallest building until 1913 when the Woolworth Building was completed at 792 feet. Sara Teasdale's poem, "The Woolworth Tower," takes her reader to the top of the tower to discuss human insignificance compared to the size and longevity of the buildings in the city. In 1908, Frank Winfield Woolworth wanted a building to serve as the headquarters of his company and the Irving National Bank. This structure became the Woolworth Building. It is located on 233 Broadway, and it remained the world's tallest building until 1930. Winfield clearly wanted the public to be impressed with this building, and Teasdale's poem reveals that she was.

New forms of transportation such as subways and taxis also inspired poets. Amy Lowell writes about a taxi taking her farther and farther away from someone she wants to be close to in her poem "The Taxi." The narrator's ride makes her feel lonely and gloomy. In early 1907, Henry N. Allen imported 65 gasoline-powered vehicles from France and started the New York Taxicab company. The vehicles were green and red, but Allen repainted them yellow so that they could be visible from a distance. By 1908, his company had 700 taxis on the street. The fare was 50 cents a mile, equivalent to about fourteen dollars and fourteen cents in 2019, a rate only relatively wealthy people could pay. As a result, the subway was created because the city was crowded, and not everyone could afford a taxi. Dana Burnet questions subway riders' worth morally, socially, and financially in her poem "Subway Track-Walkers." She could not have done this if the first Interborough Rapid Transit subway line had not opened on October 27, 1904. The line ran from City Hall station to 145th street, and a ride cost five cents, equivalent to 2 dollars and thirty-six cents in 2019.

When the Brooklyn Bridge was completed in 1883, it further changed transportation in the city. The bridge connects lower Manhattan to Brooklyn over the East River. Richard Le Gallienne, in his poem "Brooklyn Bridge at Dawn," writes, "Who, seeing thus the bridge a-slumber there / would dream such softness, like a picture hung / is wrought of human thunder, iron and blood." The narrator of the poem questions how such a beautiful, delicate-looking structure could possibly hurt the people who were working on it as much as it did. John Roebling dreamed of constructing the Brooklyn Bridge as early as the 1850s when he began drawing designs of it. However, construction did not begin until 1869. Sadly, shortly after construction began, Roebling was surveying the Brooklyn side of the East River and a boat ran into the ferry slip where he was standing, crushing his right foot. Roebling died shortly after this accident from tetanus. Roebling's son, Washington, took over the construction. The building process depended upon caissons, large wooden boxes with no bottoms. Workers had to dig out the riverbed in order for the caissons to sink low enough to build the bridge's foundation. The caissons on the Brooklyn side of the bridge had to sink to a depth of

44 feet, while the caissons on the Manhattan side had to sink to 78 feet. These boxes were poorly ventilated, lit by gas lamps, and filled with pressurized air. A leak in the wood, a problem with the air pumps, or a fire could cause the box to depressurize, make the water rise, or create another crisis that could kill everyone inside.

If caisson workers moved too quickly out of the compressed air, they got "Caisson disease" or "the bends." Symptoms include, but are not limited to, headache, fatigue, nausea, joint and limb pain, confusion, unconsciousness, heart problems, resperatory problems, and rashes. The symptoms vary depending on where gas bubbles form in the body. This disease struck many workers, and it crippled Washington. He stayed at his home in Brooklyn while construction continued, and his wife, Emily, carried messages between him and his workers. Emily became a respectable engineer and designer as the bridge was being finished. At least twenty workers died during the construction from various causes such as falling, fires, or the bends. The bridge opened with a huge celebration on May 24, 1883. It was by far the longest suspension bridge in the world with a main span of 1,595.5 feet. It would be surpassed by the Williamsburg Bridge in 1903 with a main span of 1,600 feet.

New methods of transportation and the creation of bridges made people rely less on the ferry for transportation, but some people rode it for fun. Edna St. Vincent Millay, in her poem "Recuerdo," writes about her narrator having a great time riding the ferry all night. The narrator gives money along with some apples and pears to a woman. The tone is cheerful and shows that riding the ferry will make someone "merry" and inspire generosity. In 1814, Robert Fulton introduced steam-powered vessels to the New York Harbor, south of Manhattan, to expand settlement across the East River. This invention created small businesses that ran their own ferry rides. The Brooklyn Union Ferry Company then bought the rights to the ferry system from these businesses. In the 1850s, the company had seven routes with 40,000,000 annual customers. However, as tunnels and bridges were being built in the late 1800s and early 1900s, fewer people relied on ferries for transport between the boroughs. Thus, the city began taking over the failing companies with support from public investment in vessels and terminals. By the 1920s, New York had an extensive municipal ferry system.

Although industrialization made travel easier, it also created unsafe jobs with poor pay. In "At Dawn," George Cabot Lodge comments on the fact that corporation owners care more about gaining money than other people's lives. He criticizes the person who profits from employees working so hard they lose their soul, and he attempts to get the reader to sympathize with the worker in his poem. In the cramped Triangle Waist Garment Factory, immigrant women and teenagers worked in unsafe conditions. Near closing time on March 25, 1911, a fire broke out in the factory, killing 146 people who had no way to escape. The fire spread from the eighth to the tenth floor, and the only fire escape collapsed during the rescue effort. Many of the workers were trapped by long tables and bulky machines. Workers also struggled to flee the fire because managers had locked doors to prevent theft, and some doors opened the wrong way. This tragedy brought a renewed sense of urgency to the labor movement and to other groups working to improve women's and immigrants' rights in the workplace. The boss's indifference to the safety of workers was one of the moral issues that caused Lodge to write, "All that the soul has lost and greed has won."

Immigrants flooded into New York creating over-population. Ellis Island opened on January 1, 1892 for processing immigrants entering the United States. The facility is in the Upper New York Bay, east of Liberty State Park, and just north of Liberty Island. The most immigrants—1.25 million of them—came through Ellis Island in 1907. The foreign-born population of New York City grew from 1,270,080 in 1900 to 2,028,160 by 1920. In his poem "Sea-gulls of Manhattan," Henry Van-Dyke comments on feeling trapped in the city because people are around him all the time and he lack access to nature. Thomas Augustine Daly's poem, "Een Napoli," can be read as mocking Italian immigrants for missing their home country and complaining about work. Daly himself was Irish and picked up on different accents of people while working in a grocery store in his native Philadelphia. The poem is offensive and bigoted in its representation of Italians in New York, but it is included in this anthology to show stereotypes of the time.

Between 1881 and 1911, almost 1.5 million Jewish people fled Europe to escape religious persecution. Maxwell Bodenheim powerfully depicts a Jewish man who has lost his soul, hopes, dreams, and beliefs to the Ghetto on the East Side of New York in his poem, "East Side: New York." The piece creates a grave image of the old man, and the last line —"the Ghetto walks away with him"— reveals how he has lost his soul and goals. Lola Ridge's book *The Ghetto and Other Poems* explores Jewish lives in the city. The narrator of the title poem describes her roach-infested room on the fifth floor as being "bare" and having "coppery stains" on her "low ceiling[s]" and "green plaster walls." The Ghettos of the East Side were crowded, unsafe, and unclean. By 1900, there were 700 people per acre living on the East Side, causing diseases and fires. Jewish people also worked long hours for meager wages. This connects to Bodenheim's poem where he writes that workers had, "thwarted longings in life." Most Jewish people did not have the opportunity to accomplish what they truly wanted to in the city. They either worked in sweatshops, started their own businesses, worked in the garment industry and retail sales, or were peddlers. Lola Ridge casually writes of "Bodies dangl[ing] from the fire escapes" to show how often dead and sick people were seen in the crowded Ghetto.

Although Manhattan housed the Jewish Ghettos, poets were still inspired by Manhattan's beauty. Edwin Curran boldly calls Manhattan "God's own city of the western world," and he describes Manhattan as holding up heaven in his poem, "Manhattan." Curran admires the immortality of Manhattan in this poem along with its beauty. Also included in this anthology is Charles Hanson Towne's book of poems, *Manhattan*, in which he shows his love and hate for the borough. He is indifferent to Manhattan because it feels like home, but it also traps him. Manhattan was the entire city of New York until 1898 when it annexed the Bronx, Brooklyn, Queens, and Richmond. In 1900, Manhattan held 54% of New York City's population, even though it had only 8% of New York City's total land mass. The population of Manhattan in 1900 was 1,850,093, while the population of New York City as a whole was 3,437,202. The island is also the smallest borough of the City at 22.7 square miles. Although Manhattan is small, it contains numerous locations that have inspired artists including Gramercy Park, Bowling Green, Battery Park, Central Park, The Metropolitan Museum, Wall Street, and Harlem.

Broadway is another popular setting in early twentieth-century poetry. Herman Hagedorn's "The Peddler" expands on the idea that everyone in Broadway has a duty to their city. The peddler sells pencils on the same corner of Broadway that he has for the past twenty years. He provides a service for everyone in the city, and he has observed the people on Broadway his whole career. Thus, the peddler informs the reader what he thinks of the people he has watched for so long. Sara Teasdale's narrator speaks about taking full advantage of the night in her poem "Broadway." Teasdale writes, "A somber man drifts by, and only we / Pass up the street unwearied, warm and free." She shows that Broadway has other pleasures to offer than theaters, such as simply walking down the street with friends. The Theater District of Broadway encompasses the area around 42nd street to 53rd street in Midtown and from 6th to 8th avenues. Broadway had about twenty theaters in 1900, and this number grew to a high of eighty in 1925. The theaters used bright electric white signs to advertise shows, which led to Broadway receiving the nickname "The Great White Way." Teasdale's setting reveals that these bright signs drown out the stars.

While the city was modernizing, new literary movements emerged. Ezra Pound developed Imagism around 1900. He said that an image "is the presentation of such a 'complex' instantaneously which gives the sense of sudden liberation; that sense of freedom from time limits and space limits; that sense of sudden growth, which we experience in the presence of the greatest works of art." Sara Teasdale, another imagist writer, presents the image of the buildings around Central Park right before spring in her poem, "Central Park at Dusk." The buildings represent the growth in the city, and the image of a silent woman waiting for love represents the quietness of the scene. The image of the lady is also used to show the time of year. Following Pound's definition, Teasdale treats the scene directly, and every word in the poem musically describes the scene. Amy Lowell also dabbled in imagism until she concluded that Pound's outlook was too nearsighted, lacking creativity and intelligence. In 1915 she had been the leader of the movement, but she steered away from it in 1917. She started writing with unrestricted rhyme instead of focusing on images. Imagists included in this anthology along with Amy Lowell and Sara Teasdale are William Carlos Williams, Lola Ridge, and Charles Hanson Towne.

The Harlem Renaissance was another important early twentieth-century literary movement in which African Americans in Harlem found a distinct voice and identity. When the United States entered World War I, many African Americans traveled north to take on jobs that were previously exclusive to white men. African American employment created an environment in which art could thrive. They made jazz, blues, dance, theater, art, fiction, and poetry. Major poets of this time period include Langston Hughes, Claude McKay, Countee Cullen, and James Weldon Johnson. Claude McKay writes about a girl losing her true self and the ownership of her body to prostitution as she dances provocatively in his poem, "The Harlem Dancer." He again comments on black prostitutes in "Harlem Shadows" to reveal the degradation of the entire black community. In "The City's Love," McKay's narrator says there is a "moment rare" when he forgets that he is a black man in the city. Although McKay can sometimes lose himself in the city, he shows he still misses his birthplace of Jamaica in his poem "The Tropics in New York."

The diversity of poets included in this anthology provides a variety of outlooks on the dramatically changing city. Dana Burnet questions the morality of people on the subways, while Vachel Lindsay admires Broadway's electrical signs. Louise Morgan Smith Sill misses Maiden Lane before it was modernized, and Evelyn Scott feels that she lost her true-self to the crowd moving about the city. The poets present widely different themes and attitudes in their writing, but together they capture the vibrancy and complexity of New York City in the early twentieth century.

Hannah Watt
April 2019

Bibliography

"Amy Lowell." *Poetry Foundation*, www.poetryfoundation.org/poets/amy-lowell.

"A Brief Guide to Imagism." *Poets.org*, Academy of American Poets, 5 Sept. 2017, www.poets.org/poetsorg/text/brief-guide-imagism.

"Broadway." *Encyclopaedia Britannica Inc.*, 18 Mar. 2019, www.britannica.com/topic/Broadway-street-and-district-New-York-City.

"Ellis Island History." *The Statue of Liberty-Ellis Island Foundation Inc.*, 2019, libertyellisfoundation.org/ellis-island-history.

"The Evolution (and New Revolution) of New York Ferry Service." *Ferry*, www.ferry.nyc/wp-content/uploads/2017/02/The-Evolution-and-New-Revolution-of-New-York-Ferry-Service.pdf.

Guzenfeld, Inna. "The Evolution (and New Revolution) of NYC's Ferry Service; Citywide Ferry to Launch Summer 2017." *Untapped Cities*, 19 Jan. 2017, untappedcities.com/2017/01/09/the-evolution-and-new-revolution-of-nycs-ferry-service-citywide-ferry-to-launch-summer-2017/.

"A History of the New York Cab." *Telegraph Media Group*, 4 May 2011, www.telegraph.co.uk/news/worldnews/northamerica/usa/8491507/A-history-of-the-New-York-cab.html.

"Immigration: Polish and Russian." *Library of Congress*, www.loc.gov/teachers/classroommaterials/presentationsandactivities/presentations/immigration/polish6.html.

Maher, James. "Brooklyn Bridge History and Photography." *James Maher Photography*, 4 Mar. 2016, www.jamesmaherphotography.com/new-york-historical-articles/brooklyn-bridge/.

Matlins, Melissa. "Metropolitan Life Building." *Skyscraper*, www.skyscraper.org/TALLEST_TOWERS/t_metro.htm.

McLaren, Nicholas. "All About Decompression Sickness." *ThoughtCo*, 11 Feb. 2019, www.thoughtco.com/all-about-decompression-sickness-2963035.

McNamara, Robert. "Building the Brooklyn Bridge." *ThoughtCo*, 10 Jan. 2019, www.thoughtco.com/building-the-brooklyn-bridge-1773695.

"Metropolitan Life Clock Tower." *Flatiron District*, www.flatirondistrict.nyc/discover-flatiron/flatiron-history/1/metropolitan-life-clock-tower.

NYC, www1.nyc.gov/assets/planning/download/pdf/data-maps/nyc-population/historical-population/nyc_total_pop_1900-2010.pdf.

NYC, www1.nyc.gov/assets/planning/download/pdf/data-maps/nyc-population/historical-population/1790-2000_nyc_total_foreign_birth.pdf.

Sutton, Philip. "The Woolworth Building: The Cathedral of Commerce." *The New York Public Library*, 22 Apr. 2013, www.nypl.org/blog/2013/04/22/woolworth-building-cathedral-commerce.

"Manhattan." *Encyclopaedia Britannica Inc.*, www.britannica.com/place/Manhattan-New-York-City.

"Thomas Augustine Daly." *All Poetry*, allpoetry.com/Thomas-Augustine-Daly.

"Today in History - June 12." *The Library of Congress*, www.loc.gov/item/today-in-history/june-12/.

"The Triangle Shirtwaist Factory Fire." *Occupational Safety & Health Administration*, www.osha.gov/oas/trianglefactoryfire.html.

Note on the Text

I have been faithful to the original texts as much as possible. Spelling and phrasings were preserved in order to maintain the authenticity of the texts.

Claude McKay

The White City

I will not toy with it nor bend an inch.
Deep in the secret chambers of my heart
I muse my life-long hate, and without flinch
I bear it nobly as I live my part.
My being would be a skeleton, a shell,
If this dark Passion that fills my every mood,
And makes my heaven in the white world's hell,
Did not forever feed me vital blood.
I see the mighty city through a mist--
The strident trains that speed the goaded mass,
The poles and spires and towers vapor-kissed,
The fortressed port through which the great shipspass,
The tides, the wharves, the dens I contemplate,
Are sweet like wanton loves because I hate.

Dawn in New York

The Dawn! The Dawn! The crimson-tinted, comes
Out of the low still skies, over the hills,
Manhattan's roofs and spires and cheerless domes!
The Dawn! My spirit to its spirit thrills.
Almost the mighty city is asleep,
No pushing crowd, no tramping, tramping feet.
But here and there a few cars groaning creep
Along, above, and underneath the street,
Bearing their strangely-ghostly burdens by,
The women and the men of garish nights,
Their eyes wine-weakened and their clothes awry,

Grotesques beneath the strong electric lights.
The shadows wane. The Dawn comes to New York.
And I go darkly-rebel to my work.

The City's Love

For one brief golden moment rare like wine,
The gracious city swept across the line;
Oblivious of the color of my skin,
Forgetting that I was an alien guest,
She bent to me, my hostile heart to win,
Caught me in passion to her pillowy breast;
The great, proud city, seized with a strange love,
Bowed down for one flame hour my pride to prove.

The Tropics in New York

Bananas ripe and green, and ginger-root,
    Cocoa in pods and alligator pears,
And tangerines and mangoes and grape fruit,
    Fit for the highest prize at parish fairs,

Set in the window, bringing memories
    Of fruit-trees laden by low-singing rills,
And dewy dawns, and mystical blue skies
    In benediction over nun-like hills.

My eyes grew dim, and I could no more gaze;
    A wave of longing through my body swept,
And, hungry for the old, familiar ways,
    I turned aside and bowed my head and wept.

On Broadway

About me young and careless feet
Linger along the garish street;
Above, a hundred shouting signs
Shed down their bright fantastic glow
Upon the merry crowd and lines
Of moving carriages below.
Oh wonderful is Broadway—only
My heart, my heart is lonely.

Desire naked, linked with Passion,
Goes strutting by in brazen fashion;
From playhouse, cabaret and inn
The rainbow lights of Broadway blaze
All gay without, all glad within;
As in a dream I stand and gaze
At Broadway, shining Broadway—only
My heart, my heart is lonely.

Harlem Shadows

I hear the halting footsteps of a lass
    In Negro Harlem when the night lets fall
Its veil. I see the shapes of girls who pass
    To bend and barter at desire's call.
Ah, little dark girls who in slippered feet
Go prowling through the night from street to street!

Through the long night until the silver break
    Of day the little gray feet know no rest;
Through the lone night until the last snow-flake

3

Has dropped from heaven upon the earth's
      white breast,
The dusky, half-clad girls of tired feet
Are trudging, thinly shod, from street to street.

Ah, stern harsh world, that in the wretched way
      Of poverty, dishonor and disgrace,
Has pushed the timid little feet of clay,
      The sacred brown feet of my fallen race!
Ah, heart of me, the weary, weary feet
In Harlem wandering from street to street.

The Harlem Dancer

Applauding youths laughed with young prostitutes
And watched her perfect, half-clothed body sway;
Her voice was like the sound of blended flutes
Blown by black players upon a picnic day.
She sang and danced on gracefully and calm,
The light gauze hanging loose about her form;
To me she seemed a proudly-swaying palm
Grown lovelier for passing through a storm.
Upon her swarthy neck black shiny curls
Luxuriant fell; and tossing coins in praise,
The wine-flushed, bold-eyed boys, and even the girls,
Devoured her shape with eager, passionate gaze;
But looking at her falsely-smiling face,
I knew her self was not in that strange place.

Subway Wind

Far down, down through the city's great, gaunt gut
    The gray train rushing bears the weary wind;
In the packed cars the fans the crowd's breath cut,
    Leaving the sick and heavy air behind.
And pale-cheeked children seek the upper door
    To give their summer jackets to the breeze;
Their laugh is swallowed in the deafening roar
    Of captive wind that moans for fields and seas;
Seas cooling warm where native schooners drift
    Through sleepy waters, while gulls wheel and
        sweep,
Waiting for windy waves the keels to lift
    Lightly among the islands of the deep;
Islands of lofty palm trees blooming white
    That lend their perfume to the tropic sea,
Where fields lie idle in the dew drenched night,
    And the Trades float above them fresh and free.

When Dawn Comes to the City

The tired cars go grumbling by,
    The moaning, groaning cars,
And the old milk carts go rumbling by
    Under the same dull stars.
Out of the tenements, cold as stone,
    Dark figures start for work;
I watch them sadly shuffle on,
    'Tis dawn, dawn in New York.

But I would be on the island of the sea,

In the heart of the island of the sea,
     Where the cocks are crowing, crowing, crowing,
     And the hens are cackling in the rose-apple tree,
   Where the old draft-horse is neighing, neighing,
neighing,
          Out on the brown dew-silvered lawn,
     And the tethered cow is lowing, lowing, lowing,
   And dear old Ned is braying, braying, braying,
   And the shaggy Nannie goat is calling, calling,
calling
        From her little trampled corner of the long wide
          lea
     That stretches to the waters of the hill-stream
          falling
          Sheer upon the flat rocks joyously!
          There, oh, there! on the island of the sea,
            There would I be at dawn.

The tired cars go grumbling by,
          The crazy, lazy cars,
     And the same milk carts go rumbling by
          Under the dying stars.
     A lonely newsboy hurries by,
          Humming a recent ditty;
     Red streaks strike through the gray of the sky,
          The dawn comes to the city.

          But I would be on the island of the sea,
          In the heart of the island of the sea,
     Where the cocks are crowing, crowing, crowing,
     And the hens are cackling in the rose-apple tree,
   Where the old draft-horse is neighing, neighing,
          neighing
          Out on the brown dew-silvered lawn,

And the tethered cow is lowing, lowing, lowing,
And dear old Ned is braying, braying, braying,
And the shaggy Nannie goat is calling, calling,
     calling,
  From her little trampled corner of the long wide
       lea
That stretches to the waters of the hill-stream
     falling
     Sheer upon the flat rocks joyously!
     There, oh, there! on the island of the sea,
       There I would be at dawn.

William Carlos Wlliams

The Great Figure

Among the rain
and lights
I saw the figure 5
in gold
on a red
firetruck
moving
with weight and urgency
tense
unheeded
to gong clangs
siren howls
and wheels rumbling
through the dark city.

Spouts

In this world of
as fine a pair of breasts
as ever I saw
the fountain in
Madison Square
spouts up of water
a white tree
that dies and lives
as the rocking water
in the basin
turns from the stonerim
back upon the jet
and rising there
reflectively drops down again.

Charles Reznikoff

From Poems
(Untitled)

On the Brooklyn Bridge I saw a man drop dead,
It meant no more than if he were a sparrow.

Above us rose Mahattan,
Below the river spread to meet bay and sky.

Edna St. Vincent Millay

Recuerdo

We were very tired, we were very merry—
We had gone back and forth all night on the ferry.
It was bare and bright, and smelled like a stable—
But we looked into a fire, we leaned across a table,
We lay on a hill-top underneath the moon;
And the whistles kept blowing, and the dawn came
soon.

We were very tired, we were very merry—
We had gone back and forth all night on the ferry;
And you ate an apple, and I ate a pear,
From a dozen of each we had bought somewhere;
And the sky went wan, and the wind came cold,
And the sun rose dripping, a bucketful of gold.

We were very tired, we were very merry,
We had gone back and forth all night on the ferry.
We hailed, "Good morrow, mother!" to a shawl-covered
head,
And bought a morning paper, which neither of us read;
And she wept, "God bless you!" for the apples and pears,
And we gave her all our money but our subway fares.

City Trees

The trees along this city street,
Save for the traffic and the trains,
Would make a sound as thin and sweet
As trees in country lanes.

And people standing in their shade
    Out of a shower, undoubtedly
Would hear such music as is made
    Upon a country tree.

Oh, little leaves that are so dumb
    Against the shrieking city air,
I watch you when the wind has come,
    I know what sound is there.

From Renascence: And Other Poems

V

If I should learn, in some quite casual way,
    That you were gone, not to return again-
Read from the back-page of a paper, say,
    Held by neighbor in a subway train,
How at the corner of this avenue
    And such a street (so are the papers filled)
A hurrying man--who happened to be you--
    At noon to-day had happened to be killed,
I should not cry aloud--I could not cry
    Aloud, or wring my hands in such a place--
I should but watch the station lights rush by

With a more careful interest on my face,
Or raise my eyes and read with greater care
Where to store furs and how to treat hair

Maxwell Bodenheim

New York City

New York, it would be easy to revile
The flatly carnal beggar in your smile,
And flagellate, with a superior bliss,
The gasping routines of your avarice.
Loud men reward you with an obvious ax,
Or piteous laurel-wreath, and their attacks
And eulogies bled to a common sin.
New York, perhaps an intellectual grin
That brings its bright cohesion to the warm
Confusion of the heart, can mold your swarm
Of huge, drab bunders into smaller grace . . .
With old words I shall gamble for your face.

The evening kneels between your filthy brink,
Darkly indifferent to each scheme and trick
With which your men insult and smudge their day.
When evenings metaphysically pray
Above the weakening dance of men, they find
That every eye that looks at them is blind.
And yet, New York, I say that evenings free
An insolently mystic majesty
From your parades of automatic greed.
For one dark moment all your narrow speed
Receives the fighting blackness of a soul,
And every nervous lie swings to a whole—
A pilgrim, blurred yet proud, who finds in black
An arrogance that fills his straining lack.
Between your undistinguished crates of stone
And wood, the wounded dwarfs who walked alone—

The chorus-girls, whose indiscretions hang
Between the scavengers of rouge and slang;
The women moulding painfully a fresh
Excuse for pliant treacheries of flesh;

The men who raise the tin sword of a creed,
Convinced that it can kill the lunge of greed;
The thieves whose poisoned vanity purloins
A fancied victory from ringing coins;
The staidly bloated men whose minds have sold
Their quickness to an old, metallic Scold;
The neatly cultured men whose hopes and fears
Dwell in soft prisons honored by past years;
The men whose tortured youth bends to the task
Of hardening offal to a swaggering mask —
The night, with black hands, gathers each mistake
And strokes a mystic challenge from each ache.
The night, New York, sardonic and alert,
Offers a soul to your reluctant dirt.

City Streets

This pavement and the sordid boast of stone
And brick that wins the pity of a sky
Are only martyred symbols made to buy
A dream of permanence for flesh and bone.
The jumbled, furtive anecdotes of lips
And limbs that bring their fever to this street,
They will subside to fragments of defeat
Within the cool republic where death trips.

This is an age where flesh desires to shape
Intense hyperboles in prose and verse,

Transforming city streets and country lanes
To backgrounds aiding physical escape.
But city streets are waiting to disperse
With ruins the fight and plight of earthly pains.

Summer Evening: New York Subway-Station

Perspiring violence derides
The pathetic collapse of dirt.
An effervescence of noises
Depends upon cement for its madness.
Electric light is taut and dull,
Like a nauseated suspense.
This kind of heat is the recollection
Of an orgy in a swamp.
Soiled caskets joined together
Slide to rasping stand-stills.
People savagely tamper
With each other's bodies,
Scampering in and out of doorways.
Weighted with apathetic bales of people
The soiled caskets rattle on.
The scene consists of mosaics
Jerkily pieced together and blown apart.
A symbol of billowing torment,
This sturdy girl leans against an iron girder.
Weariness has loosened her face
With its shining cruelty.
Round and poverty-stricken
Her face renounces life.
Her white cotton waist is a wet skin on her breast:
Her black hat, crisp and delicate,
Does not understand her head.

An old man stoops beside her,
Sweat and wrinkles errupting
Upon the blunt remnants of his face.
A little black pot of a hat
Corrupts his grey-haired head.

Two figures on a subway-platform,
Pieced together by an old complaint

Broadway

With sardonic futility
The multi-coloured crowd,
Hurried by fervent sensuality,
Flees from something carried on its back.
Endlessly subdued, a sound
Pours up from the crowd,
Like some one ever gasping for breath
To utter releasing words.
Through the artificial valley
Made by gaudy evasions,
The stifled crowd files up and down,
Stabbing thought with rapid noises.
Women strutting dulcetly,
Embroider their unappeased hungers,
And men stumble toward a flitting opiate.
Sometimes a moment breaks apart
And one can hear the knuckles
Of children rapping on towering doors:
Rapping on the highway
Where civilization parades
Its frozen amiabilities!

East-Side: New York

An old Jew munches an apple,
With conquering immersion
All the thwarted longings of his life
Urge on his determined teeth.
His face is hard and pear-shaped;
His eyes are muddy capitulations;
But his mouth is incongruous.
Softly, slightly distended,
Like that of a whistling girl,
It is ingenuously haunting
And makes the rest of him a soiled, grey background.
Hopes that lie within their grave
Of submissive sternness,
Have spilled their troubled ghosts upon this mouth,
And a tortured belief
Has dwindled into tenderness upon it . . .
He trudges off behind hid push-cart
And the Ghetto walks away with him.

Fifth Avenue
(New York)

Seasons bring nothing to this gulch
Save a harshly intimate anecdote
Scrawled, here and there, on paint and stone.
The houses shoulder each other
In a forced and passionless communication.
Their harassed angles rise
Like a violent picture-puzzle
Hiding a story that only ruins could reveal;

Their straight lines, robbed of power,
Meet in dwarfed rebellion.
Sometimes they stand like vastly flattened faces
Suffering ants to crawl
In and out of their gaping mouths.
Sometimes, in menial attitudes
They stand like Gothic platitudes
Slipshodly carved in dark brown stone.
Tarnished solemnities of death
Cast their transfigured hue on this avenue.
The cool and indiscriminate glare
Of sunlight seems to desecrate a tomb,
And the racing people seem
A stream of accidental shadows.
Hard noises strike one's face and make
It numb with momentary reality,
But the noiseless undertone returns
And they change to unreal jests
Made by death.

Evelyn Scott

Ascension: Autumn Dusk in Central Park

Featureless people glide with dim motion through a
     quivering blue silver;
Boats merge with the bronze-gold welters about their
     keels.
The trees float upward in gray and green flames.
Clouds, swans, boats, trees, all gliding up a hillside
After some gray old women who lift their gaunt forms
From falling shrouds of leaves.

Thin fingered twigs clutch darkly at nothing.
Crackling skeletons shine.
Along the smutted horizon of Fifth Avenue
The hooded houses watch heavily
With oily gold eyes.

From Brooklyn

Along the shore
A black net of branches
Tangles the pulpy yellow lamps.
The shell-colored sky is lustrous with the fading sun.
Across the river Manhattan floats —
Dim gardens of fire —
And rushing invisible toward me through the fog,
A hurricane of faces.

Midnight Worship: Brooklyn Bridge

In the rain
Rows of street lamps are saints in bright garments
That flow long with the bend of knees.
They lift pale heads nimbussed with golden spikes.

Up the lanes of liquid onyx
Toward the high fire-laden altars
Move the saints of Manhattan
In endless pilgrimage to death,
Amidst the asphodel and anemones of dawn.

Potter's Field

Golden petals, honey sweet,
Crushed beneath fear-hastened feet . . .

Silver paper lanterns glow and shudder
In flat patterns
On a gray eternal face
Stained with pain.

New York

With huge diaphanous feet,
March the leaden velvet elephants,
Pressing the bodies back into the earth.

Sunset: Battery Park

From cliffs of houses,
Sunlit windows gaze down upon me
Like undeniable eyes,
Millions of bronze eyes,
Unassailable,
Obliterating all they see:
The warm contiguous crowd in the street below
Chills,
Mists,
Drifts past those hungry eyes of Eternity,
Melts seaward and deathward
To the ocean.

Summer Night

The bloated moon
Has sickly leaves glistening against her
Like flies on a fat white face.

The thick-witted drunkard on the park bench
Touches a girl's breast
That throbs with its own ruthless and stupid delight.
The new-born child crawls in his mother's filth.
Life, the sleep walker,
Lifts toward the skies
An immense gesture of indecency.

Crowds

The sky along the street a gauzy yellow:
The narrow lights burn tall in the twilight.

The cool air sags,
Heavy with the thickness of bodies.
I am elated with bodies.
They have stolen me from myself.
I love the way they beat me to life,
Pay me for their cruelties.
In the close intimacy I feel for them
There is the indecency I like.
I belong to them,
To these whom I hate;
And because we can never know each other,
Or be anything to each other,
Though we have been the most,
I sell so much of me that could bring a better price.

The City at Night

Life wriggles in and out
Through the narrow ways
And circuitous passages:
Something monstrous and horrible,
A passion without any master,
Male sexual fluid trickling through the darkness
And setting fire to whatever it touches.

That is the master
Bestowing a casual caress on a slave.
Quiver under it!

Lola Ridge

The Ghetto

I

Cool, inaccessible air
Is floating in velvety blackness shot with steel-blue
    lights,
But no breath stirs the heat
Leaning its ponderous bulk upon the Ghetto
And most on Hester street . . .

The heat . . .
Nosing in the body's overflow,
Like a beast pressing its great steaming belly close,
Covering all avenues of air . . .

The heat in Hester street,
Heaped like a dray
With the garbage of the world.

Bodies dangle from the fire escapes
Or sprawl over the stoops . . .
Upturned faces glimmer pallidly—
Herring-yellow faces, spotted as with a mold,
And moist faces of girls
Like dank white lilies,
And infants' faces with open parched mouths
    that suck at the air as at empty teats.

Young women pass in groups,
Converging to the forums and meeting halls,

Surging indomitable, slow
Through the gross underbrush of heat.
Their heads are uncovered to the stars,
And they call to the young men and to one another
With a free camaraderie.
Only their eyes are ancient and alone . . .

The street crawls undulant,
Like a river addled
With its hot tide of flesh
That ever thickens.
Heavy surges of flesh
Break over the pavements,
Clavering like a surf—
Flesh of this abiding
Brood of those ancient mothers who saw the dawn
    break over Egypt . . .
And turned their cakes upon the dry hot stones
And went on
Till the gold of the Egyptians fell down off their
    arms . . .
Fasting and athirst . . .
And yet on . . .

Did they vision—with those eyes darkly clear,
That looked the sun in the face and were not blinded—
Across the centuries
The march of their enduring flesh?
Did they hear—
Under the molten silence
Of the desert like a stopped wheel—
(And the scorpions tick-ticking on the sand . . .)
The infinite procession of those feet?

II

I room at Sodos'—in the little green room that was
    Bennie's—
With Sadie
And her old father and her mother,
Who is not so old and wears her own hair.

Old Sodos no longer makes saddles.
He has forgotten how.
He has forgotten most things—even Bennie who stays
    away and sends wine on holidays—
And he does not like Sadie's mother
Who hides God's candles,
Nor Sadie
Whose young pagan breath puts out the light—
That should burn always,
Like Aaron's before the Lord.

Time spins like a crazy dial in his brain,
And night by night
I see the love-gesture of his arm
In its green-greasy coat-sleeve
Circling the Book,
And the candles gleaming starkly
On the blotched-paper whiteness of his face,
Like a miswritten psalm . . .
Night by night
I hear his lifted praise,
Like a broken whinnying
Before the Lord's shut gate.

Sadie dresses in black.
She has black-wet hair full of cold lights
And a fine-drawn face, too white.
All day the power machines
Drone in her ears . . .
All day the fine dust flies
Till throats are parched and itch
And the heat—like a kept corpse—
Fouls to the last corner.

Then—when needles move more slowly on the cloth
And sweaty fingers slacken
And hair falls in damp wisps over the eyes—
Sped by some power within,
Sadie quivers like a rod . . .
A thin black piston flying,
One with her machine.

She—who stabs the piece-work with her bitter eye
And bids the girls: "Slow down—
You'll have him cutting us again!"
She—fiery static atom,
Held in place by the fierce pressure all about—
Speeds up the driven wheels
And biting steel—that twice
Has nipped her to the bone.

Nights, she reads
Those books that have most unset thought,
New-poured and malleable,
To which her thought
Leaps fusing at white heat,
Or spits her fire out in some dim manger of a hall,
Or at a protest meeting on the Square,

Her lit eyes kindling the mob . . .
Or dances madly at a festival.
Each dawn finds her a little whiter,
Though up and keyed to the long day,
Alert, yet weary . . . like a bird
That all night long has beat about a light.

The Gentile lover, that she charms and shrews,
Is one more pebble in the pack
For Sadie's mother,
Who greets him with her narrowed eyes
That hold some welcome back.
"What's to be done?" she'll say,
"When Sadie wants she takes . . .
Better than Bennie with his Christian woman . . .
A man is not so like,
If they should fight,
To call her Jew . . ."

Yet when she lies in bed
And the soft babble of their talk comes to her
And the silences . . .
I know she never sleeps
Till the keen draught blowing up the empty hall
Edges through her transom
And she hears his foot on the first stairs.

Sarah and Anna live on the floor above.
Sarah is swarthy and ill-dressed.
Life for her has no ritual.
She would break an ideal like an egg for the winged
    thing at the core.
Her mind is hard and brilliant and cutting like an
    acetylene torch.

If any impurities drift there, they must be burnt up as
    in a clear flame.
It is droll that she should work in a pants factory.
—Yet where else . . . tousled and collar awry at her
    olive throat.
Besides her hands are unkempt.
With English . . . and everything . . . there is so little
    time.
She reads without bias—
Doubting clamorously—
Psychology, plays, science, philosophies—
Those giant flowers that have bloomed and withered,
    scattering their seed . . .
—And out of this young forcing soil what growth may
come—what amazing blossomings.

Anna is different.
One is always aware of Anna, and the young men turn
    their heads to look at her.
She has the appeal of a folk-song
And her cheap clothes are always in rhythm.
When the strike was on she gave half her pay.
She would give anything—save the praise that is hers
And the love of her lyric body.

But Sarah's desire covets nothing apart.
She would share all things . . .
Even her lover.

III

The sturdy Ghetto children
March by the parade,

Waving their toy flags,
Prancing to the bugles—
Lusty, unafraid . . .
Shaking little fire sticks
At the night—
The old blinking night—
Swerving out of the way,
Wrapped in her darkness like a shawl.

But a small girl
Cowers apart.
Her braided head,
Shiny as a black-bird's
In the gleam of the torch-light,
Is poised as for flight.
Her eyes have the glow
Of darkened lights.

She stammers in Yiddish,
But I do not understand,
And there flits across her face
A shadow
As of a drawn blind.
I give her an orange,
Large and golden,
And she looks at it blankly.
I take her little cold hand and try to draw her to me,
But she is stiff . . .
Like a doll . . .

Suddenly she darts through the crowd
Like a little white panic
Blown along the night—
Away from the terror of oncoming feet . . .

And drums rattling like curses in red roaring mouths . . .
And torches spluttering silver fire
And lights that nose out hiding-places . . .
To the night—
Squatting like a hunchback
Under the curved stoop—
The old mammy-night
That has outlived beauty and knows the ways of fear—
The night—wide-opening crooked and comforting
    arms,
Hiding her as in a voluminous skirt.

The sturdy Ghetto children
March by the parade,
Waving their toy flags,
Prancing to the bugles,
Lusty, unafraid.
But I see a white frock
And eyes like hooded lights
Out of the shadow of pogroms
Watching . . . watching . . .

IV

Calicoes and furs,
Pocket-books and scarfs,
Razor strops and knives
(Patterns in check . . .)

Olive hands and russet head,
Pickles red and coppery,
Green pickles, brown pickles,
(Patterns in tapestry . . .)

31

Coral beads, blue beads,
Beads of pearl and amber,
Gewgaws, beauty pins—
Bijoutry for chits—
Darting rays of violet,
Amethyst and jade . . .
All the colors out to play,
Jumbled iridescently . . .
(Patterns in stained glass
Shivered into bits!)

Nooses of gay ribbon
Tugging at one's sleeve,
Dainty little garters
Hanging out their sign . . .
Here a pout of frilly things—
There a sonsy feather . . .
(White beards, black beards
Like knots in the weave . . .)

And ah, the little babies—
Shiny black-eyed babies—
(Half a million pink toes
Wriggling altogether.)
Baskets full of babies
Like grapes on a vine.

Mothers waddling in and out,
Making all things right—
Picking up the slipped threads
In Grand street at night—
Grand street like a great bazaar,
Crowded like a float,

Bulging like a crazy quilt
Stretched on a line.

But nearer seen
This litter of the East
Takes on a garbled majesty.

The herded stalls
In dissolute array . . .
The glitter and the jumbled finery
And strangely juxtaposed
Cans, paper, rags
And colors decomposing,
Faded like old hair,
With flashes of barbaric hues
And eyes of mystery . . .
Flung
Like an ancient tapestry of motley weave
Upon the open wall of this new land.

Here, a tawny-headed girl . . .
Lemons in a greenish broth
And a huge earthen bowl
By a bronzed merchant
With a tall black lamb's wool cap upon his head . . .
He has no glance for her.
His thrifty eyes
Bend—glittering, intent
Their hoarded looks
Upon his merchandise,
As though it were some splendid cloth
Or sumptuous raiment
Stitched in gold and red...

He seldom talks
Save of the goods he spreads—
The meager cotton with its dismal flower—
But with his skinny hands
That hover like two hawks
Above some luscious meat,
He fingers lovingly each calico,
As though it were a gorgeous shawl,
Or costly vesture
Wrought in silken thread,
Or strange bright carpet
Made for sandaled feet . . .

Here an old grey scholar stands.
His brooding eyes—
That hold long vistas without end
Of caravans and trees and roads,
And cities dwindling in remembrance—
Bend mostly on his tapes and thread.

What if they tweak his beard—
These raw young seed of Israel
Who have no backward vision in their eyes—
And mock him as he sways
Above the sunken arches of his feet—
They find no peg to hang their taunts upon.
His soul is like a rock
That bears a front worn smooth
By the coarse friction of the sea,
And, unperturbed, he keeps his bitter peace.

What if a rigid arm and stuffed blue shape,
Backed by a nickel star
Does prod him on,

Taking his proud patience for humility . . .
All gutters are as one
To that old race that has been thrust
From off the curbstones of the world . . .
And he smiles with the pale irony
Of one who holds
The wisdom of the Talmud stored away
In his mind's lavender.

But this young trader,
Born to trade as to a caul,
Peddles the notions of the hour.
The gestures of the craft are his
And all the lore
As when to hold, withdraw, persuade, advance . . .
And be it gum or flags,
Or clean-all or the newest thing in tags,
Demand goes to him as the bee to flower.
And he—appraising
All who come and go
With his amazing
Sleight-of-mind and glance
And nimble thought
And nature balanced like the scales at nought—
Looks Westward where the trade-lights glow,
And sees his vision rise—
A tape-ruled vision,
Circumscribed in stone—
Some fifty stories to the skies.

V

As I sit in my little fifth-floor room—
Bare,
Save for bed and chair,
And coppery stains
Left by seeping rains
On the low ceiling
And green plaster walls,
Where when night falls
Golden lady-bugs
Come out of their holes,
And roaches, sepia-brown, consort . . .
I hear bells pealing
Out of the gray church at Rutgers street,
Holding its high-flung cross above the Ghetto,
And, one floor down across the court,
The parrot screaming:
Vorwärts . . . Vorwärts . . .

The parrot frowsy-white,
Everlastingly swinging
On its iron bar.

A little old woman,
With a wig of smooth black hair
Gummed about her shrunken brows,
Comes sometimes on the fire escape.
An old stooped mother,
The left shoulder low
With that uneven droopiness that women know
Who have suckled many young . . .
Yet I have seen no other than the parrot there.

I watch her mornings as she shakes her rugs
Feebly, with futile reach
And fingers without clutch.
Her thews are slack
And curved the ruined back
And flesh empurpled like old meat,
Yet each conspires
To feed those guttering fires
With which her eyes are quick.

On Friday nights
Her candles signal
Infinite fine rays
To other windows,
Coupling other lights,
Linking the tenements
Like an endless prayer.

She seems less lonely than the bird
That day by day about the dismal house
Screams out his frenzied word . . .
That night by night—
If a dog yelps
Or a cat yawls
Or a sick child whines,
Or a door screaks on its hinges,
Or a man and woman fight—
Sends his cry above the huddled roofs:
Vorwärts . . . Vorwärts . . .

VI

In this dingy café
The old men sit muffled in woollens.
Everything is faded, shabby, colorless, old . . .
The chairs, loose-jointed,
Creaking like old bones—
The tables, the waiters, the walls,
Whose mottled plaster
Blends in one tone with the old flesh.

Young life and young thought are alike barred,
And no unheralded noises jolt old nerves,
And old wheezy breaths
Pass around old thoughts, dry as snuff,
And there is no divergence and no friction
Because life is flattened and ground as by many mills.

And it is here the Committee—
Sweet-breathed and smooth of skin
And supple of spine and knee,
With shining unpouched eyes
And the blood, high-powered,
Leaping in flexible arteries—
The insolent, young, enthusiastic, undiscriminating
        Committee,
Who would placard tombstones
And scatter leaflets even in graves,
Comes trampling with sacrilegious feet!

The old men turn stiffly,
Mumbling to each other.
They are gentle and torpid and busy with eating.

But one lifts a face of clayish pallor,
There is a dull fury in his eyes, like little rusty grates.
He rises slowly,
Trembling in his many swathings like an awakened
    mummy,
Ridiculous yet terrible.
—And the Committee flings him a waste glance,
Dropping a leaflet by his plate.

A lone fire flickers in the dusty eyes.
The lips chant inaudibly.
The warped shrunken body straightens like a tree.
And he curses . . .
With uplifted arms and perished fingers,
Claw-like, clutching . . .
So centuries ago
The old men cursed Acosta,
When they, prophetic, heard upon their sepulchres
Those feet that may not halt nor turn aside for ancient
    things.

VII

Here in this room, bare like a barn,
Egos gesture one to the other—
Naked, unformed, unwinged
Egos out of the shell,
Examining, searching, devouring—
Avid alike for the flower or the dung . . .
(Having no dainty antennae for the touch and
    withdrawal—
Only the open maw . . .)

Egos cawing,
Expanding in the mean egg . . .
Little squat tailors with unkempt faces,
Pale as lard,
Fur-makers, factory-hands, shop-workers,
News-boys with battling eyes
And bodies yet vibrant with the momentum of long
    runs,
Here and there a woman . . .

Words, words, words,
Pattering like hail,
Like hail falling without aim . . .
Egos rampant,
Screaming each other down.
One motions perpetually,
Waving arms like overgrowths.
He has burning eyes and a cough
And a thin voice piping
Like a flute among trombones.

One, red-bearded, rearing
A welter of maimed face bashed in from some old
    wound,
Garbles Max Stirner.
His words knock each other like little wooden blocks.
No one heeds him,
And a lank boy with hair over his eyes
Pounds upon the table.
—He is chairman.

Egos yet in the primer,
Hearing world-voices
Chanting grand arias . . .

Majors resonant,
Stunning with sound . . .
Baffling minors
Half-heard like rain on pools . . .
Majestic discordances
Greater than harmonies . . .
—Gleaning out of it all
Passion, bewilderment, pain . . .

Egos yearning with the world-old want in their eyes—
Hurt hot eyes that do not sleep enough . . .
Striving with infinite effort,
Frustrate yet ever pursuing
The great white Liberty,
Trailing her dissolving glory over each hard-won
        barricade—
Only to fade anew . . .

Egos crying out of unkempt deeps
And waving their dreams like flags—
Multi-colored dreams,
Winged and glorious . . .

A gas jet throws a stunted flame,
Vaguely illumining the groping faces.
And through the uncurtained window
Falls the waste light of stars,
As cold as wise men's eyes . . .
Indifferent great stars,
Fortuitously glancing
At the secret meeting in this shut-in room,
Bare as a manger.

VIII

Lights go out
And the stark trunks of the factories
Melt into the drawn darkness,
Sheathing like a seamless garment.

And mothers take home their babies,
Waxen and delicately curled,
Like little potted flowers closed under the stars.

Lights go out
And the young men shut their eyes,
But life turns in them . . .

Life in the cramped ova
Tearing and rending asunder its living cells . . .
Wars, arts, discoveries, rebellions, travails, immolations,
    cataclysms, hates . . .
Pent in the shut flesh.
And the young men twist on their beds in languor and
    dizziness unsupportable . . .
Their eyes—heavy and dimmed
With dust of long oblivions in the gray pulp behind—
Staring as through a choked glass.
And they gaze at the moon—throwing off a faint heat—
The moon, blond and burning, creeping to their cots
Softly, as on naked feet . . .
Lolling on the coverlet . . . like a woman offering her
    white body.

Nude glory of the moon!
That leaps like an athlete on the bosoms of the young

girls stripped of their linens;
Stroking their breasts that are smooth and cool as
    mother-of-pearl
Till the nipples tingle and burn as though little lips
    plucked at them.
They shudder and grow faint.
And their ears are filled as with a delirious rhapsody,
That Life, like a drunken player,
Strikes out of their clear white bodies
As out of ivory keys.

Lights go out . . .
And the great lovers linger in little groups, still
    passionately debating,
Or one may walk in silence, listening only to the still
    summons of Life—
Life making the great Demand . . .
Calling its new Christs . . .
Till tears come, blurring the stars
That grow tender and comforting like the eyes of
    comrades;
And the moon rolls behind the Battery
Like a word molten out of the mouth of God.

Lights go out . . .
And colors rush together,
Fusing and floating away . . .
Pale worn gold like the settings of old jewels . . .
Mauves, exquisite, tremulous, and luminous purples
And burning spires in aureoles of light
Like shimmering auras.

They are covering up the pushcarts . . .
Now all have gone save an old man with mirrors—

Little oval mirrors like tiny pools.
He shuffles up a darkened street
And the moon burnishes his mirrors till they shine like
    phosphorus . . .
The moon like a skull,
Staring out of eyeless sockets at the old men trundling
    home the pushcarts.

IX

A sallow dawn is in the sky
As I enter my little green room.
Sadie's light is still burning . . .
Without, the frail moon
Worn to a silvery tissue,
Throws a faint glamour on the roofs,
And down the shadowy spires
Lights tip-toe out . . .
Softly as when lovers close street doors.

Out of the Battery
A little wind
Stirs idly—as an arm
Trails over a boat's side in dalliance—
Rippling the smooth dead surface of the heat,
And Hester street,
Like a forlorn woman over-born
By many babies at her teats,
Turns on her trampled bed to meet the day.

LIFE!
Startling, vigorous life,
That squirms under my touch,

And baffles me when I try to examine it,
Or hurls me back without apology.
Leaving my ego ruffled and preening itself.

Life,
Articulate, shrill,
Screaming in provocative assertion,
Or out of the black and clotted gutters,
Piping in silvery thin
Sweet staccato
Of children's laughter,

Or clinging over the pushcarts
Like a litter of tiny bells
Or the jingle of silver coins,
Perpetually changing hands,
Or like the Jordan somberly
Swirling in tumultuous uncharted tides,
Surface-calm.

Electric currents of life,
Throwing off thoughts like sparks,
Glittering, disappearing,
Making unknown circuits,
Or out of spent particles stirring
Feeble contortions in old faiths
Passing before the new.

Long nights argued away
In meeting halls
Back of interminable stairways—
In Roumanian wine-shops
And little Russian tea-rooms . . .

Feet echoing through deserted streets
In the soft darkness before dawn . . .
Brows aching, throbbing, burning—
Life leaping in the shaken flesh
Like flame at an asbestos curtain.

Life—
Pent, overflowing
Stoops and facades,
Jostling, pushing, contriving,
Seething as in a great vat . . .

Bartering, changing, extorting,
Dreaming, debating, aspiring,
Astounding, indestructible
Life of the Ghetto . . .

Strong flux of life,
Like a bitter wine
Out of the bloody stills of the world . . .
Out of the Passion eternal.

Manhattan

Out of the night you burn, Manhattan,
In a vesture of gold—
Span of innumerable arcs,
Flaring and multiplying—
Gold at the uttermost circles fading
Into the tenderest hint of jade,
Or fusing in tremulous twilight blues,
Robing the far-flung offices,
Scintillant-storied, forking flame,

Or soaring to luminous amethyst
Over the steeples aureoled—

Diaphanous gold,
Veiling the Woolworth, argently
Rising slender and stark
Mellifluous-shrill as a vender's cry,
And towers squatting graven and cold
On the velvet bales of the dark,
And the Singer's appraising
Indolent idol's eye,
And night like a purple cloth unrolled—

Nebulous gold
Throwing an ephemeral glory about life's vanishing
    points,
Wherein you burn . . .
You of unknown voltage
Whirling on your axis . . .
Scrawling vermillion signatures
Over the night's velvet hoarding . . .
Insolent, towering spherical
To apices ever shifting.

Broadway

Light!
Innumerable ions of light,
Kindling, irradiating,
All to their foci tending . . .

Light that jingles like anklet chains
On bevies of little lithe twinkling feet,

Or clingles in myriad vibrations
Like trillions of porcelain
Vases shattering . . .

Light over the laminae of roofs,
Diffusing in shimmering nebulæ
About the night's boundaries,
Or billowing in pearly foam
Submerging the low-lying stars . . .

Light for the feast prolonged—
Captive light in the goblets quivering . . .
Sparks evanescent
Struck of meeting looks—
Fringéd eyelids leashing
Sheathed and leaping lights . . .
Infinite bubbles of light
Bursting, reforming . . .
Silvery filings of light
Incessantly falling . . .
Scintillant, sided dust of light
Out of the white flares of Broadway—
Like a great spurious diamond
In the night's corsage faceted . . .

Broadway,
In ambuscades of light,
Drawing the charmed multitudes
With the slow suction of her breath—
Dangling her naked soul
Behind the blinding gold of eunuch lights
That wind about her like a bodyguard.

Or like a huge serpent, iridescent-scaled,

Trailing her coruscating length
Over the night prostrate—
Triumphant poised,
Her hydra heads above the avenues,
Values appraising
And her avid eyes
Glistening with eternal watchfulness . . .

Broadway—
Out of her towers rampant,
Like an unsubtle courtezan
Reserving nought for some adventurous night.

Brooklyn Bridge

Pythoness body—arching
Over the night like an ecstasy—
I feel your coils tightening . . .
And the world's loosening breath.

Wall Street at Night

Long vast shapes . . . cooled and flushed through with
    darkness. . . .
Lidless windows
Glazed with a flashy luster
From some little pert café chirping up like a sparrow
And down amoung iron guts
Piled silver
Throwing gray spatter of light . . . pale without heat . . .
Like the pallor of deas bodies.

East River

Dour river
Jaded with monotony of lights
Diving off mast heads . . .
Lights mad with creating in a river . . . turning its sullen
    back . . .
Heave up, river . . .
Vomit back into the darkness your spawn of light. . . .
The night will gut what you give her.

Skyscrapers

Skyscrapers . . . remote, unpartisan . . .
Turning neither to the right nor left
Your imperturbable fronts . . .
Austerely greeting the sun
With one chilly finger of stone . . .
I know your secrets . . . better than all the policemen
    like fat blue mullet along the avenues.

Sara Teasdale

Broadway

This is the quiet hour; the theaters
    Have gathered in their crowds, and steadily
    The million lights blaze on for few to see,
Robbing the sky of stars that should be hers.
A woman waits with bag and shabby furs,
  A somber man drifts by, and only we
  Pass up the street unwearied, warm and free,
For over us the olden magic stirs.
Beneath the liquid splendor of the lights
  We live a little ere the charm is spent;
This night is ours, of all the golden nights,
    The pavement an enchanted palace floor,
And Youth the player on the viol, who sent
    A strain of music thru an open door.

Spring

In Central Park the lovers sit,
    On every hilly path they stroll,
Each thinks his love is infinite,
    And crowns his soul.

But we are cynical and wise,
    We walk a careful foot apart,
You make a little joke that tries
    To hide your heart.

Give over, we have laughed enough;
    Oh dearest and most foolish friend,
Why do you wage a war with love
    To lose your battle in the end?

The Old Maid

I saw her in a Broadway car,
    The woman I might grow to be;
I felt my lover look at her
    And then turn suddenly to me.

Her hair was dull and drew no light
    And yet its color was as mine;
Her eyes were strangely like my eyes
    Tho' love had never made them shine.

Her body was a thing grown thin,
    Hungry for love that never came;
Her soul was frozen in the dark
    Unwarmed forever by love's flame.

I felt my lover look at her
    And then turn suddenly to me,—
His eyes were magic to defy
    The woman I shall never be.

From the Woolworth Tower

Vivid with love, eager for greater beauty
Out of the night we come
Into the corridor, brilliant and warm.

A metal door slides open,
And the lift receives us.
Swiftly, with sharp unswerving flight
The car shoots upward,
And the air, swirling and angry,
Howls like a hundred devils.
Past the maze of trim bronze doors,
Steadily we ascend.
I cling to you
Conscious of the chasm under us,
And a terrible whirring deafens my ears.

The flight is ended.

We pass thru a door leading onto the ledge—
Wind, night and space
Oh terrible height
Why have we sought you?
Oh bitter wind with icy invisible wings
Why do you beat us?
Why would you bear us away?
We look thru the miles of air,
The cold blue miles between us and the city,
Over the edge of eternity we look
On all the lights,
A thousand times more numerous than the stars;
Oh lines and loops of light in unwound chains
That mark for miles and miles
The vast black mazy cobweb of the streets;
Near us clusters and splashes of living gold
That change far off to bluish steel
Where the fragile lights on the Jersey shore
Tremble like drops of wind-stirred dew.
The strident noises of the city

Floating up to us
Are hallowed into whispers.
Ferries cross thru the darkness
Weaving a golden thread into the night,
Their whistles weird shadows of sound.

We feel the millions of humanity beneath us,—
The warm millions, moving under the roofs,
Consumed by their own desires;
Preparing food,
Sobbing alone in a garret,
With burning eyes bending over a needle,
Aimlessly reading the evening paper,
Dancing in the naked light of the café,
Laying out the dead,
Bringing a child to birth—
The sorrow, the torpor, the bitterness, the frail joy
Come up to us
Like a cold fog wrapping us round.
Oh in a hundred years
Not one of these blood-warm bodies
But will be worthless as clay.
The anguish, the torpor, the toil
Will have passed to other millions
Consumed by the same desires.
Ages will come and go,
Darkness will blot the lights
And the tower will be laid on the earth.
The sea will remain
Black and unchanging,
The stars will look down
Brilliant and unconcerned.

Beloved,
Tho' sorrow, futility, defeat
Surround us,
They cannot bear us down.
Here on the abyss of eternity
Love has crowned us
For a moment
Victors.

At Night

We are apart; the city grows quiet between us,
　　She hushes herself, for midnight makes heavy her
　　　　eyes,
The tangle of traffic is ended, the cars are empty,
　　Five streets divide us, and on them the moonlight
　　　　lies.

Oh are you asleep, or lying awake, my lover?
　　Open your dreams to my love and your heart to my
　　　　words,
I send you my thoughts-the air between us is laden,
　　My thoughts fly in at your window, a flock of wild
　　　　birds.

New Year's Dawn—Broadway

When the horns wear thin
And the noise, like a garment outworn,
Falls from the night,
The tattered and shivering night,
That thinks she is gay;

When the patient silence comes back,
And retires,
And returns,
Rebuffed by a ribald song,
Wounded by vehement cries,
Fleeing again to the stars—
Ashamed of her sister the night;
Oh, then they steal home,
The blinded, the pitiful ones
With their gew-gaws still in their hands,
Reeling with odorous breath
And thick, coarse words on their tongues.
They get them to bed, somehow,
And sleep the forgiving,
Comes thru the scattering tumult
And closes their eyes.
The stars sink down ashamed
And the dawn awakes,
Like a youth who steals from a brothel,
Dizzy and sick.

The Lights Of New York

The lightning spun your garment for the night
    Of silver filaments with fire shot thru,
    A broidery of lamps that lit for you
The steadfast splendor of enduring light.
The moon drifts dimly in the heaven's height,
    Watching with wonder how the earth she knew
    That lay so long wrapped deep in dark and dew,
Should wear upon her breast a star so white.
The festivals of Babylon were dark
    With flaring flambeaux that the wind blew down;

The Saturnalia were a wild boy's lark
    With rain-quenched torches dripping thru the town—
But you have found a god and filched from him
A fire that neither wind nor rain can dim.

Union Square

With the man I love who loves me not,
    I walked in the street-lamps' flare;
We watched the world go home that night
    In a flood through Union Square.

I leaned to catch the words he said
    That were light as a snowflake falling;
Ah well that he never leaned to hear
    The words my heart was calling.

And on we walked and on we walked
    Past the fiery lights of the picture shows—
Where the girls with thirsty eyes go by
    On the errand each man knows.

And on we walked and on we walked,
    At the door at last we said good-bye;
I knew by his smile he had not heard
    My heart's unuttered cry.

With the man I love who loves me not
    I walked in the street-lamps' flare—
But oh, the girls who ask for love
    In the lights of Union Square.

Summer Night, Riverside

In the wild, soft summer darkness
How many and many a night we two together
Sat in the park and watched the Hudson
Wearing her lights like golden spangles
Glinting on black satin.
The rail along the curving pathway
Was low in a happy place to let us cross,
And down the hill a tree that dripped with bloom
Sheltered us,
While your kisses and the flowers,
Falling, Falling,
Tangled my hair. . . .

The frail white stars moved slowly over the sky.

And now, far off
In the fragrant darkness
The tree is tremulous again with bloom,
For June comes back.

To-night what girl
Dreamily before her mirror shakes from her hair
This year's blossoms, clinging in its coils?

Evening: New York

Blue dust of evening over my city,
   Over the ocean of roofs and the tall towers
Where the window-lights, myriads and myriads,
   Bloom from the walls like climbing flowers.

In a Subway Station

After a year I came again to the place;
The tireless lights and the reverberation,
The angry thunder of trains that burrow the ground,
The hunted, hurrying people were still the same—
But oh, another man beside me and not you!
Another voice and other eyes in mine!
And suddenly I turned and saw again
The gleaming curve of tracks, the bridge above—
They were burned deep into my heart before,
The night I watched them to avoid your eyes,
When you were saying, "Oh, look up at me!"
When you were saying, "Will you never love me?"
And when I answered with a lie. Oh then
You dropped your eyes. I felt your utter pain.
I would have died to say the truth to you.

After a year I came again to the place—
The hunted hurrying people were still the same. . . .

The Metropolitan Tower

We walked together in the dusk
    To watch the tower grow dimly white,
And saw it lift against the sky
    Its flower of amber light.

You talked of half a hundred things,
    I kept each little word you said;
And when at last the hour was full,
    I saw the light turn red.

You did not know the time had come,
  You did not see the sudden flower,
Nor know that in my heart Love's birth
  Was reckoned from that hour.

Grammercy Park

The little park was filled with peace,
  The walks were carpeted with snow,
But every iron gate was locked.
  Lest if we entered, peace would go.

We circled it a dozen times,
  The wind was blowing from the sea,
I only felt your restless eyes
  Whose love was like a cloak for me.

Oh heavy gates that fate has locked
  To bar the joy we may not win,
Peace would go out forever
  If we should dare to enter in.

In the Metropolitan Museum

Inside the tiny Pantheon
  We stood together silently,
Leaving the restless crowd awhile
  As ships find shelter from the sea.

The ancient centuries came back
  To cover us a moment's space,

And through the dome the light was glad
    Because it shone upon your face.

Ah, not from Rome but farther still
    Beyond sun-smitten Salamis,
The moment took us, till you learned
    To find the present with a kiss.

Central Park at Dusk

Buildings above the leafless trees
    Loom high as castles in a dream,
While one by one the lamps come out
    To thread the twilight with a gleam.

There is no sign of leaf or bud,
    A hush is over everything—
Silent as women wait for love,
    The world is waiting for the spring.

Dana Burnet

Roses in the Subway

A wan-cheeked girl with faded eyes
  Came stumbling down the crowded car,
Clutching her burden to her breast
  As though she held a star.

Roses, I swear it! Red and sweet
  And struggling from her pinched white hands,
Roses . . . like captured hostages
  From far and fairy lands!

The thunder of the rushing train
  Was like a hush. . . . The flower scent
Breathed faintly on the stale, whirled air
  Like some dim sacrament—

I saw a garden stretching out
  And morning on it like a crown—
And o'er a bed of crimson bloom
  My mother . . . stooping down.

Subway Track-Walkers

Who are ye hopeless who go with dull faces,
  Treading the terrible floorways of night?
Oft have I seen ye flick by in the shadow,
  Framed from the dark by a flutter of light.

Do ye gaze up at the hurtling windows,

Streaking your dusk-world with sudden bright
  lanes?
Do ye dream dreams of the lights and the faces?
  Do ye think thoughts of the eyes at the panes?

Far is the path through the burrows of darkness!
  Fearful the death if ye falter or blunder!
Once I saw one of you caught in the whirlwind,
  Hurled to his fathers with steel and great thunder. . . .

What is your vision, and where is your meaning?
  Do ye walk only for Saturday's pay?
Or are ye sent for a desperate service
  That I may ride my true love to-day?

Washington Square

'Twas a long-ago summer when Romance and I
  Came trudging to Washington Square,
And, oh, what a laughter illuminated the walls
  Of our room at the top of the stair—
Our poor little, odd little jest of a room
  At the top of the boarding-house stair!

Laughter, and Youth, and a heart for the game,
The short road to Love, and the long road to Fame;
And all roads before us and all roads to dare,
And that was the glory of Washington Square!

Romance was twenty and I was no more,
  And there was a window, you see,
That gave us the park and a bit of sky,
  And sometimes a breath from the sea;

And small, ragged children would pause in their play
    To laugh up at Romance and me.

Children, and Wind, and the blue sky above,
The drear road to Fame, and the dear road to Love;
And all roads beginning and all roads to dare,
And that was the wonder of Washington Square!

I think I was painting the face of a dream,
    And Romance was posing in red,
And daylight was only the throb of my heart,
    And the tremble of sun on her head,
And twilight was only the sound of her voice,
    And the sense of a radiance fled.

Twilight, and Dawn, and the dream without name,
The fair road to Love, and the far road to Fame;
The star of her face and the light of her hair,
And that was the vision of Washington Square.

The gold of earth's giving has lain in my purse,
    Of laurel I've taken my share—
But where is the laughter that hallowed our room
    At the top of the boarding-house stair?
And where are the Children, and where is the Dream
    That led me to Washington Square?

Laughter, and Youth, and a heart for the game,
The old road to Love, and the bold road to Fame;
And all roads beginning and all roads to dare,
And that was the glory of Washington Square!

The Unemployed

They did not ask for lordly things,
  For temples or for lands;
They ony asked the right to use
  The glory of their hands.

I never saw a sadder thing
  Beneath God's vaulted blue
Than that grim line of starving men
  Who had no task to do.

They came before the frozen stars
  Had faded from the sky,
And all day long the wealthy folk
  Rolled curiously by.

And all day long the waiting line
  Stood shaking in the street.
And, oh, their willing, idle hands!
  And, oh, their aching feet!

I never saw a sadder thing
  In all the City's strife
Than that worn host of ragged men
  Who waited there for life.

They did not ask for alms of gold,
  Nor things of lordly worth.
They only asked the right to share
  The labor of the earth.

The Woolworth Building

I am one of the things at your feet,
   I have laughter and hope and tears—
But you have the Clouds and the Wind,
   And the hallowed defiance of years.

You are stuff of the dreams that I dream;
   You are Beauty, made tall and white,
And you live with your foot on the rock,
   And your face to the fountains of light!

I am part of the world at your feet,
   I have sorrow and laughter days,
But you have unmesurable dawns,
   And the firmness outlasting the phase.

You are God in a sermon of stone,
   The dim God that we search at your feet
You are faith lifted unto the stars,
   But we do not look up from our street.

We do not look up from our tears,
   To call you divine as we go;
But you are the temple we built,
   And then did not know, did not know!

Vachel Lindsay

A Rhyme about an Electrical Sign

I look on the specious electrical light
Blatant, mechanical, crawling and white,
Wickedly red or malignantly green
Like the beads of a young Senegambian queen.
Showing, while millions of souls hurry on,
The virtues of collars, from sunset till dawn,
By dart or by tumble of whirl within whirl,
Starting new fads for the shame-weary girl,
By maggotry motions in sickening line
Proclaiming a hat or a soup or a wine,
While there far above the steep cliffs of the street
The stars sing a message elusive and sweet.

Now man cannot rest in his pleasure and toil
His clumsy contraptions of coil upon coil
Till the thing he invents, in its use and its range,
Leads on to the marvelous CHANGE BEYOND CHANGE
Some day this old Broadway shall climb to the skies,
As a ribbon of cloud on a soul-wind shall rise.
And we shall be lifted, rejoicing by night,
Till we join with the planets who choir their delight.
The signs in the street and the signs in the skies
Shall make me a Zodiac, guiding the wise,
And Broadway make one with that marvelous stair
That is climbed by the rainbow-clad spirits of prayer.

Amy Lowell

New York at Night

A near horizon whose sharp jags
   Cut brutally into a sky
Of leaden heaviness, and crags
Of houses lift their masonry
   Ugly and foul, and chimneys lie
And snort, outlined against the gray
   Of lowhung cloud. I hear the sigh
The goaded city gives, not day
Nor night can ease her heart, her anguished labours
     stay.

Below, straight streets, monotonous,
   From north and south, from east and west,
Stretch glittering; and luminous
   Above, one tower tops the rest
   And holds aloft man's constant quest:
Time! Joyless emblem of the greed
   Of millions, robber of the best
Which earth can give, the vulgar creed
Has seared upon the night its flaming ruthless screed.

O Night! Whose soothing presence brings
   The quiet shining of the stars.
O Night! Whose cloak of darkness clings
   So intimately close that scars
   Are hid from our own eyes. Beggars
By day, our wealth is having night
   To burn our souls before altars
Dim and tree-shadowed, where the light

Is shed from a young moon, mysteriously bright.

Where art thou hiding, where thy peace?
  This is the hour, but thou art not.
Will waking tumult never cease?
  Hast thou thy votary forgot?
  Nature forsakes this man-begot
And festering wilderness, and now
  The long still hours are here, no jot
Of dear communing do I know;
Instead the glaring, man-filled city groans below!

The Taxi

When I go away from you
The world beats dead
Like a slackened drum.
I call out for you against the jutted stars
And shout into the ridges of the wind.
Streets coming fast,
One after the other,
Wedge you away from me,
And the lamps of the city prick my eyes
So that I can no longer see your face.
Why should I leave you,
To wound myself upon the sharp edges of the night?

Anticipation

I have been temperate always,
But I am like to be very drunk
With your coming.

There have been times
I feared to walk down the street
Lest I should reel with the wine of you,
And jerk against my neighbors
As they go by.
I am parched now, and my tongue is horrible in my
    mouth,
But my brain is noisy
With the clash and gurgle of filling wine-cups.

Hermann Hagedorn

Broadway

How like the stars are these white, nameless faces!
　These far innumerable burning coals!
This pale procession out of stellar spaces,
　This Milky Way of souls!
Each in its own bright nebulæ enfurled,
Each face, dear God, a world!

I fling my gaze out through the silent night—
　In those far stars, what gardens, what high halls,
Has mortal yearning built for its delight,
　What chasms and what walls?
What quiet mansions where a soul may dwell?
What heaven and what hell?

The Peddler

I peddles pencils on Broadway.
　I know it ain't a great career.
It's dull an' footless—so folks say—
　And yet I've done it twenty year,
Held down my same old corner here
　An' never missed a day.

I peddles, an' I watch the crowd.
　I knows 'em—all they say an' do—
As if they shouted it out loud
　I look 'em through an' through an' through!
By crabs! they'd kill me if they knew—

They are so fine an' proud.

I knows 'em! Oh it's in their eyes,
    It's in their walk, it's in their lips!
They tries to bluff it—but I'm wise!
    An' they're just children when you strips
The smirk off; an' the clerks, the chips,
    Stands clean of all the lies.

I've watched so long, I scarcely see
    The clo'es—it's just the faces now.
Somehow I knows their misery
    An' wonders—when? An' where? An' how?
Elbow an' shoulder—on they plough—
    An' yet somehow they speaks to me.

I'm like the priest—an' all day long
    They tells me what they've thought an' done.
An' some is flabby, some is strong,
    An' some of 'em was dead an' gone
Before they ever saw the sun. . . .
    I knows where some of 'em belong.

I peddles pencils. Christ! An' they?
    They does the things that seems worth while.
I watch 'em growin' old an' gray,
    An' queer about the eyes, an' smile
To see 'em when they've made their pile,
    A-totterin' up Broadway.

Richard Le Gallienne

Brooklyn Bridge at Dawn

Out of the cleansing night of stars and tides,
  Building itself anew in the slow dawn,
  The long sea-city rises: night is gone,
Day is not yet; still merciful, she hides
Her summoning brow, and still the night-car glides
  Empty of faces; the night-watchmen yawn
  One to the other, and shiver and pass on,
Nor yet a soul over the great bridge rides.

Frail as a gossamer, a thing of air,
  A bow of shadow o'er the river flung,
    Its sleepy masts and lonely lapping flood;
Who, seeing thus the bridge a-slumber there,
  Would dream such softness, like a picture hung,
    Is wrought of human thunder, iron and blood?

George Cabot Lodge

Lower New York
Before Dawn

Time has no spectacle more stern and strange;
   Life has no sleep so dense as that which lies
   On walls and windows, blank as sightless eyes,
   On court and prison, warehouse and exchange.
Earth has no silence such as fills the range
   Of streets left bare beneath the haughty skies: —
   Of unremembered human miseries
   Churned without purpose in the trough of change.
For here where day by day the tide-race rolls
   Of sordid greed and passions mean and blind,
   Here is a vast necropolis of souls!
And life that waits as with suspended breath,
   Weary and still, here seems more dead than death,
   Aimless and empty as an idiot's mind.

At Dawn

Here is the dawn a hopeless thing to see:
   Sordid and pale as is the face of one
   Who sinks exhausted in oblivion
   After a night of deep debauchery.
Here, as the light reveals relentlessly
   All that the soul has lost and greed has won,
   Scarce we believe that somewhere now the sun
   Dawns overseas in stainless majesty.
Yet the day comes!—ghastly and harsh and thin
   Down the cold street; and now, from far away,

We hear a vast and sullen rumor run,
As of the tides of ocean turning in. . . .
And know, for yet another human day,
The world's dull, dreadful labor is begun!

Henry VanDyke

Hudson's Last Voyage
The Shallop on Hudson Bay
June 22, 1611

One sail in sight upon the lonely sea,
And only one! For never ship but mine
Has dared these waters. We were first,
My men, to battle in between the bergs
And floes to these wide waves. This gulf is mine;
I name it! and that flying sail is mine!
And there, hull-down below that flying sail,
The ship that staggers home is mine, mine, mine!
My ship *Discoverie!*
                    The sullen dogs
Of mutineers, the bitches' whelps that snatched
Their food and bit the hand that nourished them,
Have stolen her. You ingrate Henry Greene,
I picked you from the gutter of Houndsditch,
And paid your debts, and kept you in my house,
And brought you here to make a man of you!
You Robert Juet, ancient, crafty man,
Toothless and tremulous, how many times
Have I employed you as a master's mate
To give you bread? And you Abacuck Prickett,
You sailor-clerk, you salted puritan,
You knew the plot and silently agreed,
Salving your conscience with a pious lie!
Yes, all of you—hounds, rebels, thieves! Bring back
My ship!
            Too late,—I rave,—they cannot hear
My voice: and if they heard, a drunken laugh

Would be their answer; for their minds have caught
The fatal firmness of the fool's resolve,
That looks like courage but is only fear.
They'll blunder on, and lose my ship, and drown,—
Or blunder home to England and be hanged.
Their skeletons will rattle in the chains
Of some tall gibbet on the Channel cliffs,
While passing mariners look up and say:
"Those are the rotten bones of Hudson's men
"Who left their captain in the frozen North!"

O God of justice, why hast Thou ordained
Plans of the wise and actions of the brave
Dependent on the aid of fools and cowards?

Look,—there she goes,—her topsails in the sun
Gleam from the ragged ocean edge, and drop
Clean out of sight! So let the traitors go
Clean out of mind! We'll think of braver things!
Come closer in the boat, my friends. John King,
You take the tiller, keep her head nor'west.
You Philip Staffe, the only one who chose
Freely to share our little shallop's fate,
Rather than travel in the hell-bound ship,—
Too good an English sailor to desert
These crippled comrades,—try to make them rest
More easy on the thwarts. And John, my son,
My little shipmate, come and lean your head
Against my knee. Do you remember still
That April morn in Ethelburga's church,
Five years ago, when side by side we kneeled
To take the sacrament with all our men,
Before the *Hopewell* left St. Catherine's docks
On our first voyage? It was then I vowed

My sailor-soul and years to search the sea
Until we found the water-path that leads
From Europe into Asia.
                              I believe
That God has poured the ocean round His world,
Not to divide, but to unite the lands.
And all the English captains that have dared
In little ships to plough uncharted waves,—
Davis and Drake, Hawkins and Frobisher,
Raleigh and Gilbert,—all the other names,—
Are written in the chivalry of God
As men who served His purpose. I would claim
A place among that knighthood of the sea;
And I have earned it, though my quest should fail!
For, mark me well, the honour of our life
Derives from this: to have a certain aim
Before us always, which our will must seek
Amid the peril of uncertain ways.
Then, though we miss the goal, our search is crowned
With courage, and we find along our path
A rich reward of unexpected things.
Press towards the aim: take fortune as it fares!

I know not why, but something in my heart
Has always whispered, "Westward seek your goal!"
Three times they sent me east, but still I turned
The bowsprit west, and felt among the floes
Of ruttling ice along the Greenland coast,
And down the rugged shore of Newfoundland,
And past the rocky capes and wooded bays
Where Gosnold sailed,—like one who feels his way
With outstretched hand across a darkened room,—
I groped among the inlets and the isles,
To find the passage to the Land of Spice.

I have not found it yet,—but I have found
Things worth the finding!
                              Son, have you forgot
Those mellow autumn days, two years ago,
When first we sent our little ship *Half-Moon*,—
The flag of Holland floating at her peak,—
Across a sandy bar, and sounded in
Among the channels, to a goodly bay
Where all the navies of the world could ride?
A fertile island that the redmen called
Manhattan, lay above the bay: the land
Around was bountiful and friendly fair.
But never land was fair enough to hold
The seaman from the calling of the sea.
And so we bore to westward of the isle,
Along a mighty inlet, where the tide
Was troubled by a downward-flowing flood
That seemed to come from far away,—perhaps
From some mysterious gulf of Tartary?
Inland we held our course; by palisades
Of naked rock; by rolling hills adorned
With forests rich in timber for great ships;
Through narrows where the mountains shut us in
With frowning cliffs that seemed to bar the stream;
And then through open reaches where the banks
Sloped to the water gently, with their fields
Of corn and lentils smiling in the sun.
Ten days we voyaged through that placid land,
Until we came to shoals, and sent a boat
Upstream to find,—what I already knew,—
We travelled on a river, not a strait.

But what a river! God has never poured
A stream more royal through a land more rich.

Even now I see it flowing in my dream,
While coming ages people it with men
Of manhood equal to the river's pride.
I see the wigwams of the redmen changed
To ample houses, and the tiny plots
Of maize and green tobacco broadened out
To prosperous farms, that spread o'er hill and dale
The many-coloured mantle of their crops.
I see the terraced vineyard on the slope
Where now the fox-grape loops its tangled vine
And cattle feeding where the red deer roam,
And wild-bees gathered into busy hives
To store the silver comb with golden sweet;
And all the promised land begins to flow
With milk and honey. Stately manors rise
Along the banks, and castles top the hills,
And little villages grow populous with trade,
Until the river runs as proudly as the Rhine,—
The thread that links a hundred towns and towers!
Now looking deeper in my dream, I see
A mighty city covering the isle
They call Manhattan, equal in her state
To all the older capitals of earth,—
The gateway city of a golden world,—
A city girt with masts, and crowned with spires,
And swarming with a million busy men,
While to her open door across the bay
The ships of all the nations flock like doves.
My name will be remembered there, the world
Will say, "This river and this isle were found
By Henry Hudson, on his way to seek
The Northwest Passage."
                        Yes, I seek it still,—
My great adventure and my guiding star!

For look ye, friends, our voyage is not done;
We hold by hope as long as life endures!
Somewhere among these floating fields of ice,
Somewhere along this westward widening bay,
Somewhere beneath this luminous northern night,
The channel opens to the Farthest East,—
I know it,—and some day a little ship
Will push her bowsprit in, and battle through!
And why not ours,—to-morrow,—who can tell?
The lucky chance awaits the fearless heart!
These are the longest days of all the year;
The world is round and God is everywhere,
And while our shallop floats we still can steer.

So point her up, John King, nor'west by north.
We 'll keep the honour of a certain aim
Amid the peril of uncertain ways,
And sail ahead, and leave the rest to God.

Sea-gulls of Manhattan

Children of the elemental mother,
    Born upon some lonely island shore
Where the wrinkled ripples run and whisper,
    Where the crested billows plunge and roar;
Long-winged, tireless roamers and adventurers,
    Fearless breasters of the wind and sea,
In the far-off solitary places
    I have seen you floating wild and free!

Here the high-built cities rise around you;
    Here the cliffs that tower east and west,
Honeycombed with human habitations,

Have no hiding for the sea-bird's nest:
Here the river flows begrimed and troubled;
 Here the hurrying, panting vessels fume,
Restless, up and down the watery highway,
 While a thousand chimneys vomit gloom.

Toil and tumult, conflict and confusion,
 Clank and clamor of the vast machine
Human hands have built for human bondage—
 Yet amid it all you float serene;
Circling, soaring, sailing, swooping lightly
 Down to glean your harvest from the wave;
In your heritage of air and water,
 You have kept the freedom Nature gave.

Even so the wild-woods of Manhattan
 Saw your wheeling flocks of white and grey;
Even so you fluttered, followed, floated,
 Round the *Half-Moon* creeping up the bay;
Even so your voices creaked and chattered,
 Laughing shrilly o'er the tidal rips,
While your black and beady eyes were glistening
 Round the sullen British prison-ships.

Children of the elemental mother,
 Fearless floaters 'mid the double blue,
From the crowded boats that cross the ferries
 Many a longing heart goes out to you.
Though the cities climb and close around us,
 Something tells us that our souls are free,
While the sea-gulls fly above the harbor,
 While the river flows to meet the sea!

James Oppenheim

The East River Bridge Market

These as by red-hot rivets are clutched to the nerve-
    live business thrilling the hour—
Here where the strings of the purse are touched the
    brain becomes a working power.

Where have I mixed in this scene before? In what
    strange world, in what strange age?
Lo, in the flesh of life's uproar these people float from
    a printed page,
Rises Isaiah, Rizpah, Ruth, prophet, and woman-in-
    love, and mother,
See where Isaiah is visioning Truth as he peddles fish
    to Abel's brother.

Worlds away and worlds behind all living worlds
    these souls assemble,
Rizpah there with her dead to mind, Ruth with her
    yearning heart a-tremble!
What to these are Wall Street's currents of electricity
    circling Earth?
What to these are Broadway's torrents of roaring work
    and rippling mirth?

By what nerve do these souls connect with the huge
    skyscraping towers of steel
That girdle Earth with their intellect, a might that
    world-end millions feel?
What place have these in the world we sense and
    glimpse in the morning paper's print?

Lost, they are lost in a world immense, and who is
    aware of their strife and stint?

And yet America's mightiest age shall be child of
    these wonderful mothers of men—
Each in her realm is queen and sage, and shall remake
    the world again—
Her babes are the masters of dim To-morrows, her
    daughters the wives and teachers to come,
Out of her woes and her infinite sorrows she breeds
    the Lincolns of the slum.

Out of the simple and common clay, out of the very
    earth of Earth,
Now, as ever, there break away sprits that feed the
    world's great dearth—
Take the startling gas-fire glow, stand, stand still,
    let me see your face!
Mother, that your strange heart might know you are
    the fount of a future race!

Manhattan, O My Home

Manhattan, O my Home, far-flash your windowed
    walls,
A tide of vast Atlantics comes crying to your calls,
A tide of glorious peoples on the sea-tide rolls,
O you are the Home of four-thousand-thousand Souls!

Of Souls, great Souls, until whose life entirely
        Is lost in Death, is lost to Earth shall never
            greatly roam
From your Streets where there beats every heart with

84

heart that meets
Manhattan, Manhattan, O my Home!

Manhattan, O my Home, hands like the hands of
mine
Set your trillion stones cemented in a City-shape
divine,
And my toil is building greater your Face I tremble of,
You are mine, O you Child of four million mortals'
love!
Four millions, four millions, who shaped your body
beautiful,
To stand on Earth and sun the seas, a light across
the foam—
Your least clerk cannot shrink your new Gopel-mandate:
Work!
Manhattan, Manhattan, O my Home!

Manhattan, O my Home, you are Workshop of the
World,
O none must gaze upon you save him whos strength
is hurled
In your giant Workshop labor, ever-rolling toward our
Goal:
As God, to sweat new Worlds out, as God, to build
the Soul!

The Soul, the Soul, which is won by Man through
laboring
As God built Worlds, as God wrought Man, and
shaped the starry dome:
In life's coil and turmoil we get God alone through toil!
Manhattan, Manhattan, O my Home!

Manhattan, O my Home, your wild grandeur is the
   booty
Spoiled of hills, yet how other than the hills your
   wonderous beauty—
Here is Man, not the prairies, here are lamps, scarce
   a star—
But than Nature, Human Nature is more beautiful by
   far!

O Nature, Man's Nature! your streets with Souls are
   undulant,
      The two-starred face, the supple limbs, the forms
         that go and come—
Here we steep our hearts deep in the floods of Soul
   that sweep—
      Manhattan, Manhattan, O my Home!

Manhattan, O my Home, face Fate with courage high
Go down in no death-melly, in no world-wreckage die,
Lead the Earth by the love, by the service that you
   render—
O tenoned be in God, O my City, all your splendor!

In God, our God! that deathless in your Destiny
Your Sprit through Earth's billions like a battle-cry may
   comb—
Labor hard toward the starred rolling glory of the
   Lord!—
      Manhattan, Manhattan, O my Home!

New York, From A Skyscraper

Up in the heights of the evening skies I see my City
    of Cities float
In sunset's golden and crimson dyes: I look, and a
    great joy clutches my throat!
Plateau of roofs by canyons crossed: windows by
    thousands fire-unfurled—
O gazing, how the heart is lost in the Deepest City
    of the World!

Red rolls the Hudson, golden the Bay: Brooklyn
    melts through horizons tall:
Deep in Broadway's starry gray I see the black
    man-insects crawl:
Cimneys smoke and glittering cars groan with tons
    of the homeward rush:
New York goes Home beneath its stars: what psalms
    of Joy float up this hush!

O sprawling City! Worlds in a world! Housing each
    strange type that is human—
Yonder a Little Italy curled—here the haunt of the
    Scarlet Woman—
The night's white Bacchanals of Broadway—the
    Ghetto pushcarts ringed with faces—
Wall Street's roar and the Plaza's play—O weltering
    focus of all Earth's races!

Walking your Night's many-nationed byways—
    brushing Sicilians and Jews and Greeks—
Meeting gaunt Bread Lines on your highways—
    watching night-clerks in your flaming peaks—

Marking your Theaters' outpour of splendor—pausing
    on doorsteps with resting Mothers—
I have marveled at Christs with their messages tender,
    their daring dream of a World of Brothers!

Brothers? What means Irish to the Greek? What the
    Ghetto to the Morningside?
How shall we weld the strong and the weak while
    millions struggle with light denied?
Yet, but to follow these Souls where they roam—
    ripping off housetops, the city's mask—
At night I should find each one in a Home, at Morn
    I should find each one at a Task!

Labor and Love, four-million divided—surely the
    millions at last are a-move—
Surely the brotherhood-slant is decided—the Social
    Labor, the Social Love!
Surely four millions of Souls close-gathered in this one
    spot must stagger the world—
O City, Earth's Furniture is Mothered and Fathered
    where your great streets feel the Man-tides hurled!

For the Souls in one car where they hang on the straps
    could send this City a-wing from the sod—
Each man is a tiny Faucet that taps the infinite
    reservoir of God!—
What if they turned the Faucet full stream?
    What if our millions to-night were aware?
What if to-morrow they built to their Dream the
    City of Brothers in laughter and prayer?

Morning in Central Park

When the morning sun
Spills his red lights among the naked trees
And one by one
The hills awaken—and like wind-played seas
Give back the music of the breeze,
When among film and tracery of boughs
Stripped by the winter's teeth,
Green glow the sun-filled pines—O Man, unhouse
Your head of human walls—get from beneath
Shut ceilings—let the skies take off the roof
Of your small room—and into the Park at seven
Go with tremendous stride—
Earth there is open wide
To the sun and the wind and the amplitude of heaven!

That Child, the World, from out the infinite night
Draws through the dark
Into the light—
And all the sacred mystery of Birth
Hovers on the Earth—
Even in the pale of the man-gardened Park
The mystery of Morn, the beauty and the splendor
Through the groves are slipping, from the boughs are
    dripping,
A miracle without us,
That yet the heart's core owns!—
Chant there the pebble-tripped waters shut in stones,
Sparrows are over the turf chirping and tripping,
And Man's World sings in a swinging circle about us!

O film of ice skimming the crystal pool!

See how it flashes in the wintry sun!
And hear the water splash!—how clean! how cool!
And behold how visible, yea, on every one,
The Silences of enormous centuries,
Brood on the rocks and the unstirring trees!

Hushed be the heart! for with the common Dawns
A music, not of Earth or Sky, repeats—
The hymns that Milton heard on singing morns,
The songs the winter sunrise sang to Keats!
Gray reeling muffled mist-voices lifted soft
Into deep Shakespeare's brain—these we may hear
In memory of English verse that oft
Sings to the unforgetting ear.
To him whose ear is tuned
To Nature's harmonies, the mighty morn
Has glories in it—glories slowly torn
Out of the heart of the World-Presence, God—
Mysteries, many-sunned and myriad-starred—
Glories like balm
To heal the wound
Of hurtful life—glories that wind an arm
Of many green fields about the tired head—
Glories that from the dead rocks leap and spread
To heart so wide, the very Earth we tread
Rolls through with a mighty shout witnessing God—
The skies themselves find room within us then—
And all the stars,
We absorb suns—and comets pulse their fires
Along the blood—and like a tide through bars
Of closing sand, out of the infinite sea
Into the bay of our being rolleth the Lord!
Lo, to our primal strength we are restored,
Lo, we are Men!

Lo, we are strong again!
This is the secret which the unblooded clerks
Roofed all the hours of waking and of sleeping
Miss—the true secret of Man's mightiest works—
Go, til through you—body and brain—is sweeping
Strength of the open skies and the open Earth—
Make all that strength your own—
Sets suns a-roll in your veins, bring worlds to birth
In the vast brain, drink up with your sprit, wealth
Of sunrise health,
Til the stature of Man suddenly grown
You feel the power of Earth fused with your own.

Cities are wildreness sculptured in stone—
Man only there is living—in the death
Of rocks Souls crowd, chanting in monotone
Of many works—go you and get the breath
Of living Creation in an enormous Earth—
An Earth roofed only by Eternity—
Feel the World-Presence, share the tumultuous birth
Of Morning—learn, not toil, but how to be—
To live, to enjoy, to divide with God the world—
To drink that strength whereby the Soul unfurled
To all her vastness, grows into a god—
Then, O come back, come back to where men plod,
Come back and bring the Earth you have annexed,
Replenish the waste city with your wealth
Of sunrise health—
Soothe the poor brains toil-troubled and perplext,
And do mighty Works—you have drawn from the
    sloping hill
Strength of strong crops—from sun-enflooded branches
Light, from morn music—now your heartstrings thrill
With power—strength from the brain avalanches—

You do the work of ten—
You are a Man mighty among Men—
And so God lowered in you and heart-released
Liveth, that love subdues your human labor
Even to the want and hunger of your neighbor—
You are to the City a ray of the Dawn in the East!

Leaving New York

As out of the pier with waving of white and roar of
    whistle the steamer drew,
That skyline rose in the evening height with a splendor
    piercing the sprit through—
West was the sun and east those towers, those towers
    glorious and serene—
The mightiest hint of human powers that ever the
    groping world has seen

Round the lower city we steamed and up and up
    under the bridges rolled—
Over the city's shoulder streamed the sunset in a
    glory of gold—
The man-black ferry, the smoke-plumes curled over
    the chimneys, the tugs a-steal,
 All were rich in a human world vast and busy and
    marvelous real.

Backs of tenements flaunted a trimming of washlines,
    babies and homes bared and blunt,
Naked boys were diving and swimming along the
    blackened waterfront,
Mighty factories stood in a splendor of chimneying
    smoke and golden river,

Streets went by and in twilight tender the air with
    humans was all a-quiver.

And seeing life rich and a millionfold the great tears
    started, the deep heart beat
With love of people and longings old, for earth was
    divine and life was sweet—
And when I was more alive than then, so really living,
    a pulsing part
Of the life of stars and earth and men, folded in
nature's world-warm heart?

Charles Hanson Towne

Manhattan

I

City I love—and hate!—how can I sing
The miracles of your might in such a mood?
How can I still the anger in my heart,
To tell of your great beauty? How dispel
The anguish I have known at your strong hands,
To whisper of your wonder? O City, how
Can I forget your loveliness, to sing
Ev'n for one hour your terror and despair?
Lo! I am of your children, and all day
Behind your granite walls, hemmed in by stone,
I struggle with my brothers, till my heart
Grows sick with sighing. Like some stricken bird,
Long since I beat upon my bars, and sought
Blessed release; but now—I only wait,
And dream, and hunger; and I sometimes think
If one should come to set my spirit free,
Would I go gladly?
                    Nay, the chains are strong
That bind me to these paves; but stronger yet
The spiritual thraldom that I know—
The madness in the blood and in the brain
That comes and grows and flourishes, until
It is a very portion of ourselves,
And teaches us to lose our youthful dream
Of God's wide gardens and His quiet woods;
And tells us to forget the ancient truths,
The little paths which sundown used to paint

With all the gorgeous color of the world.
Lost peace! lost rapturous evenings! olden dawns!
When shall I feel again your healing kiss
Upon my tired eyes?
                Not lost indeed
Is your fresh beauty—only vanished now,
While I am prisoner here a little while.

I heard a quiet voice
    Call to my aching heart;
But I did not dare rejoice,
    Lest swift it should depart,
And it said, 'Though you are captive now in the loud
  pulsing mart,

"Forget not your young days,
    The dreams untarnished still,
The simple boyhood ways,
    The music of the mill,
And O, the high, green hills of home, crowned with the
  daffodil!

"Remember, in your stress,
    The fragrant flower of youth,
The ancient loveliness,
    The wise, substantial truth.
The City is a golden lie, a serpent's awful tooth!"

II

I love to think of all the true love here,
Pillowed upon the City's throbbing breast;

Though false love stalks through mean or glowing
    streets,
The painted semblance of the dream God gave,
I know the opulent Rose of all the World
Flowers into life with each reviving day,
Is fed by tears from wells of kindliness,
And breathes its deathless perfume on the heart.
I know it lives, here, as in distant dawns
It sprang with fiery wonder when the world
Knew naught of cities; here it thrives the same
As when the first man clasped to his wild breast
The first young passionate woman; here the same
It flourishes and prospers as of old
It leaped to life and rapture every hour,
On endless plains, on hillslopes green with youth,
And in primeval forests burst in flame,
Proud of its lordly loveliness. I know
Its crimson leaves are bruised on the stones,
Its petals crushed beneath the tramping feet
Of brutal men; but only for a time
It seems to perish; lifted up again
With tenderness, it pours the old fragrance forth,
And from the lips of those who fold it close
Draws the blest sustenance it ever needs.

III

At dawn the City stirs. Her body aches
With the mad struggle of the day long dead,
And days before that ground her on their wheel.
She has not slept, for through her veins, the streets,
The tides of life have poured and rushed and beat
As swiftly as they did at Life's high noon.

All through the darkened hours a torrent swept
Down her innumerable thoroughfares,
A raging force that could not be subdued,
And robbed her of her slumber. All night long,
Shattered with pain, she sought to ease her brow
Upon the pillow of darkness—but in vain.
At length, in that strange hour before the light,
I think I heard the tired City sigh,
And heave one breath of utter weariness,
One frantic gasp that might atone for all
The sleep so mercilessly lost to her;
Then, girding all her strength, she rose, and faced
The immemorial sorrow of the day.

I saw the tired City fall in the arms of the Night,
Like a beautiful, weary woman, after the day's delight.

And she spake (I heard her whisper when the purple
     dusk came down,
A mantle from high heaven, to cover the teeming
town):—

"Mine eyes are heavy with anguish, my bleeding heart
     is oppressed,
For the burden of Life is on me, and I crave a little rest;

"A little ease from the sorrow I bore through the desperate
     day,
A surcease from my struggle and the busy noon's dismay."

But the Night with longing sought her, and crushed her to
     his heart,
And I saw the olden ardor waken and throb and start;

For the Night was her ancient lover, valient, yet cruel and
strong,
And he craved a waking woman, on whose lips there lived
a song;

He gave her wonderful jewels, long strings of glimmering
pearls,
And her eyes that had been tired gleamed now like a
beautiful girl's.

And he clasped on her throat a necklace that flashed and
shone like fire;
O proudly rose the City in imperial attire!

And she sang (she who was weary) for her glorious lover's
sake,
Though under the song I knew that her heart was like to
break;
She thrilled with the old-time passion, and laughed like
a little child;
When tears came brimming to her eyes, she brushed them
back—and smiled.

Ah! this is the spirit of woman that burns in the City's
breast—
She will turn with a laugh to her lover, forgetting her
longed-for rest;

She will sing when the King commands her, doing his
highest will—
And thus shall it be till the woman-soul and cities are
hushed and still.

IV

How punctually God's poor arise to serve
Mammon and Greed! O, day by day they take
Their tragic fate into their hearts again,
And like dumb sheep resume the well-worn paths
That lead to toil. Early the march begins,
Early the solemn phalanx fills the streets—
The giant City's very blood and life!
Look in their eyes—young eyes now old with pain;
Look in their faces lined so soon with care;
Look at their hands, already parchment, bruised
On rough machines that torture while they give
Life's breath—nay, but the shadow of Life's breath!
For this they take their way; for this they spend
The cool, clean hours of morning, and the sweet,
Reluctant hours of honeyed afternoon:—
That in the evening they may fare again
Back to dim homes, through crowds of brothers, lost
In the same awful vortex; stealing there
A broken rest, a brief oblivion
To give them strength to put their armor on
For other days they know will be the same!
For this they strive: that they may keep the mouths
Of pallid children fed with food enough
To grow to paler man- and womanhood,
And then to follow in the path they knew—
The piteous, narrow, sorrow-stricken way—
Yet wide enough to lead an army on,
Morn after morn, day after desolate day.

V

Spring comes to town like some mad girl, who runs
With silver feet upon the Avenue,
And, like Ophelia, in her tresses twines
The first young blossoms—purple violets
And golden daffodils. These are enough—
These fragile handfuls of miraculous bloom—
To make the monster City feel the Spring!
One dash of color on her dun-gray hood,
One flash of yellow near her pallid face,
And she and April are the best of friends—
Benighted town that needs a friend so much!
How she responds to that first soft caress,
And draws the hoyden Spring close to her heart,
And thrills and sings, and for one little time
Forgets the foolish panic of her sons,
Forgets her sordid merchandise and trade,
And lightly trips, while hurly-gurdies ring—
A wise old crone upon a holiday!

No Spring in any wildwood is like this!
The meadows take young April as they take
The dawn or sunset; gladly, it is true,
But without any festival at all.
Why! Spring's as common there as if she came
Each day, each hour! Why make a gala time?
Just let her in, invite her to sit down,
And that's sufficient!

                    But the Spring in town
Meets with a royal welcome that a queen

Might envy all her days. You never knew
Such preparations for one pretty girl!
The vendors herald her with lovely names—
"Lilacs!" and "Tulips!"—yes, and "Mignonette!"
And "Daffydowndillies!"—who has ever heard
A prettier word upon the human tongue?
And in the parks are spread, in proper rows,
Like Raleigh's coat, for her light feet to tread,
Carpets of green and purple, white and pink,—
Magic designs that flash to sudden life
When April's footfall sounds along the street.

The children hear her first—(they have a way
Of hearing delicate noises), and they fare
To those green islands mercifully set
In the wide City's everlasting sea.
They laugh when first the tulips lift their cups
To the blue sky; and when the crocuses
Hold up to heaven their chalices of dew,
They know that Spring has definitely come,
All madness, fragrance, carnival and joy.
Old men renew, for this blithe maiden's sake,
Their vanished youth; and the sad poor come out
To hear her laughter, flinging back at her
Their joyless mirth, repressed and hidden long.
Their tenements are caves of darkness, filled
With horrible air that leads to but one doom.
How wonderful to them the breath of Spring,
The first clear patch of blue above their heads,
The primal tide of warmth through alleys dim
And sick with old remembrance of brief days
Crowded with cold and pain and poverty!
April, your shining feet are needed here
In the dark districts where the City hives

Her palest children, famishing for you.
Speed, Hebe-like, to pour your glowing wine
Not for the gods, but for one God's sick poor,
Whose throats are parched for your delirious cup!

VI

What frightful things the City dares to do!
She draws us to her heart, as mothers will,
And nurses us until we are part of her—
Then laughs, and makes our childhood bleak and old,
Our youth a lonely flower that starves upon
The iron breast we thought would nourish it.
She leaves us—pitiless Mother!—to control
In helplessness our destiny; forgets
Her children who have come to her, so filled
With beautiful illusions and white dreams.
Unnatural monster!—thus to succor us,
Thus treacherously to catch us in her snare,
To make us love her so we dare not fly
Back to the wind-swept spaces of the West,
Or the cool, valient mornings of the North,
Or the warm, dripping, singing lanes we left
In the good Southern country. Utterly
She owns us, as a bondsman owns his slaves,
Exulting in their servitude; and we
Dare not rebel. Rather, we learn to love
The very hand that smites us! And we cling
To the great marble arms enfolding us,
And nestle closer, closer every day!

This is the iron City's awful way—
Not wilfully to crush our bodies down

Beneath her agate heel; but day by day
    To choke us with wild loneliness; to drown
Our hearts and hopes—yet never quite to slay.
This is her manner with the sons of men—
    To torture us until we bleed with pain;
Yet once her fingers clutch us, futile then
    Our hope to wipe away their crimson stain;
Nay, like poor hounds, we kiss her hand again!

She dares to fling us in her frightful tides,
Not knowing whether we can breast the waves;
She hurls us in her seething ocean, there
To fight the perilous currents as we may.
And some go down; and some, on lonely isles
Find shelter that is even worse than death.
They hear the waves—yet dare not face again
Their mighty force; and sundered from the souls
They hoped to make their brothers, they grow old
In the bleak isolation that they know.
Like lonesome rocks set in the City's sea,
Are the stone dwellings man himself has reared;
And two poor outcasts, lashed by the same storm
Of bitter circumstance, may live for years
Close to each other—yet a world apart,
Braving the same storms of adversity,
Knowing the same relentless solitude,
Yet fearing to reveal some piteous sign. . . .
What frightful things the City dares to do!

VII

A lonely girl sat in a far, high room,
The while below her, like a giant flower,

The city broke in blossom, light by light,
Until, upon this thin branch of the world,
It flaunted its wild yellow and its gold.
She heard the thunder of ten thousand hoofs,
The clang of cars, the bells and motor horns,
The rumble of the Elevated road,
The distant clamor of an ambulance
As swift upon its errand desperate,
It fought its way across a crowded street;
She saw the myriad honeycombs of light,
From towers and high hotels; and far away
The eyes of ferryboats that crawled like worms
Through the deep darkness on their changeless
        course;
And on the far-off shore beyond the town
She saw the faint, sweet lights of little homes
Where waited many a wife and many a child
For the glad coming of the one whose voice
Would crown with rapture the long, tired day.
Far, far below her, in the surging stream,
She saw, through tears, hosts of young lovers take
Their happy way along the thoroughfares;
And she could picture, though she could not see,
The laughter in their eyes and on their lips;
And she could guess the wonder in their hearts
As on they swept, like dust upon the flowers
Of the great City's magical bouquet.

Who thought of her, and many like her there,
Lost in the curious system of hotels?—
A quiet guest whom no one seemed to know,
A gentle girl who went her simple way,
Said her "Good-morning" to the passive clerks,
And spent her hours in tragic solitude;

Asked for her slender mail at eight o'clock,
Did her poor scribbling when the mood was on,
And watched the bright procession of the town
When work was not insistent. Day by day,
So went her ordered life. She could endure
The loneliness when all the world was bright
With sunshine, and she had no time to brood
On the green slopes from whence her feet had come.
But O the nights!—the flowering nights of pain,
The lamps of joy that trembled in the streets
And threw their bright reflections in her face,
And mocked her when she sat in solitude
In her dim window, awful night on night! . . .
A lonely girl sat in a far, high room.

> Alone—yet not alone
>   In this wild whirl and blur;
> How vacantly the stone
>   Stares up at her!

> Alone!—but in her heart
>   Echoes of others' myrth;
> Close, close, yet far apart,
>   O ancient earth!

> Alone—with Love so near,
>   Yet leagues and leagues away;
> No wonder that men here
>   Forget to pray!

> Alone!—No distance makes
>   Such solitude as this;
> While her heart bleeds and breaks,
>   Hearken—a kiss!

A lonely man, whose days grew lonelier still,
Fought Life upon the City's battleground,
And turned each sundown to a quiet room,
Where no one waited when his footsteps fell
Along his hotel's echoing corridor.
The Subway, that live worm beneath the ground,
Whirled him at evening to the place he called
His "home"—an empty name that chilled his heart.
The glittering halls that feigned to welcome him,
Killed the last hope of hospitality
By their aggressive grandeur; the paid smiles
Of servile bell-boys irritated him,
And the absurd politeness of the clerks
Seemed but a mockery in this fatuous world.
He was a number—not a name—to them;
He had a room on such and such a floor,
A key that corresponded with the box
Wherein they put his letters—few enough.
He might have died, and little would have cared;
He might go out and not come back again.
They'd miss him? Yes, an hour or so, perhaps,
And then, with clock-like regularity,
The wheels of the establishment would turn,
And turn, and turn; and he, who formed one cog
In the machinery so deftly oiled,
Would have his place refilled, and—that was all.

One night he saw her in the hall; her eyes
Were young, yet tired, like his; she haunted him,
And all next day, at his hot desk downtown,
He thought of her—that lonely girl whose face
Seemed beautiful and gentle; and he thought
How he would like to have her for his friend.

Yet, if he spoke, he felt she might resent
His brief "Good-evening," and refuse to take
His honest courtesy at its true worth.
Thus, often did he pass her silently. . . .
He learned to watch for her. The weeks went by,
The fleeting months, and though he sometimes saw
Her fragile figure in the dining-room
Or in the hall, he dared not speak to her,
Nor she, of course, to him. . . . Two hungry hearts,
Each aching with a nameless emptiness;
Two souls whose very silence must have said
More than a world of speech, a world of tears,
Yet destined to go on their separate ways. ...
So sped the years for her; and so for him—
A lonely man whose days grew lonelier still.

VIII

Sometimes the City, like a woman, hides
Beneath a veil, woven of silvery mist;
And sudden darkness plunges every street
In shadow and gloom. Then comes the purple rain,
Lightly at first, as if afraid to beat
Upon the web of roofs and battlements
That flaunt their challenge to the distant clouds.
A boom sounds in the Harbor. Jove's loud guns
And all the calvery of heaven have charged
Upon the solid ramparts of the town.
Bright swords of steel flash in the blackened sky,
And God's great army marches to attack
The bastions standing firm, impregnable,
Strong in their granite beauty everywhere.
Like leaden bullets falls the stinging rain,

And crash on crash the thunder's cannonade
Rolls through the armored City in its might.
O loud the martial language of the storm
Cries out in fury, and the beating hail
Hurls down its fiery shells in awful wrath.
The grim artillery of the Lord of War
Fills with dismay the cowering citizens,
Hemmed in like flies who have no sure escape.
Now, now I love your strength, O City! Now
I see your Titan power! Not that you give
Back to the elements what they have given,
But that you bravely face the rough stampede,
And stand your ground, imperishable still!
Not like a rose you droop before the gale,
But like an armored Amazon defend
Your bulwarks, till the last faint shot is fired,
And the white moon and stars come, singing peace.

From heaven's high ramparts sweeping down
The blue battallions stormed the town;
Vast regiments, an endless train,
With slanting bayonets of rain.

With fusillade and open fire
They rushed on turret, dome and spire,
And loudly with a million hoofs,
Their calvary crossed groaning roofs.

Through dripping, tear-swept panes of glass,
I saw the mighty army pass
In silent file, with solemn tramp,
Back to its far, mysterious Camp.

IX

They tear them down—the little homes—
    They cannot leave them long;
It is as if they robbed the world
    Of every little song.

Turrets and towers leap in their place,
    When frantic Commerce calls;
And underneath Trade's ruthless hand
    Each little homestead falls.

Too soon we lose them—little friends—
    Too soon their faces go;
Not Time, but man, has crushed them all,
    And laid their beauty low.

Change, change unceasing is the City's cry—
Hew down the trees in every sheltered street,
Build broader avenues and higher towers,
Stretch out into the bright suburban ways,
And snatch the distant villages and towns.
A monster centipede that swiftly stirs,
Manhattan, not content with her domain,
Reaches for far environs greedily.
She flings her bridges over waterways,
Magician-like, almost in one brief night,
And hungering for another tiny crumb,
She bores beneath the river a mighty arm,
Until she grasps a bit of countryside,
Seizing it as a spider does a fly.
Her ferryboats, like speeding envoys, keep
Patiently, tirelessly their changeless tracks,

And swing into their slips with punctual pride
Those slips that are their hourly destiny.

When will she cease this terrible desire
For larger power and greater glory? When
Will she repent of her incessant greed,
And, utterly weary of the sense of gain,
Be quite content to say, "My tasks are done;
Now I will rest awhile, for I am tired."

O, never, never will the City sing
The song of labor done; she prospers most
When toiling for the processes of Growth.
Her doom is to be greater, greater still,
Her destiny to lure the country in,
To be a portion of her blood and soul.
Her voice is like the ocean's—never hushed;
Her turbulence the waves'—it must go on;
She cannot root up now the seeds long sown,
But, driven hard by that same Fate she made,
She must press forward in the endless race.

X

The sweltering Summer brings her furious fires
And lights them on the City's iron hearth.
In the great corridors of streets, the blaze
Leaps high till every pavement trembles with heat,
As August feeds the flame from her deep store.
The rich—because our God is good to them—
Flee to the mountains' shelter or the sea,
Untroubled by the sudden waves of fire;
But the pale army of the poor must stay,

Though on their brows the scorching tongues are
   laid,
And blistering nights conspire against their rest.
The laborers march to their accustomed toil
In cavernous places where the hot sun pours
His molten beams; and on the asphalt droop
A hundred stricken horses every day.

At sunset, homeward move the dull-eyed throngs;
Some steal their broken slumber in the parks,
Some stretch upon the narrow fire-escapes,
Praying for one soft whisper of the breeze;
And the dim docks that kiss the river's edge
Are filled with families gasping for the air.
Here sits a mother with her sickly child,
There aged men pant in the livid heat,
While on the neighboring pier a raucous band
Hurls out its waltz for tireless youth to dance.

Forlorn and ragged refuse of the town,
Poor foreigners who sought our shore with hope,
Now literally upon that shore to dream
A sadly different dream from one now dead,
How my heart breaks for you this breathless night,
Swept here, unhappy derelicts, to stare,
Sleepless, while crawl the hot and tedious hours.

Here in the furnace City, in the humid air they faint,
   God's pallid poor, His people, with scarcely space for
      breath;
So foul their teeming houses, so full of shame and taint,
   They cannot crowd within them for the frightful fear of
      Death.

*Yet somewhere, Lord, Thine open seas are singing with
   the rain,*
   *And somewhere underneath Thy stars the cool waves
      crash and beat;*
*Why is it here, and only here, are huddled Death and
   Pain,*
   *And here the form of Horror stalks, a menace in the
      street!*

*The burning flagstones gleam like glass at morning and
   at noon,*
   *The giant walls shut out the breeze—if any breeze
      should blow;*
*And high above the smothering town at midnight
   hangs the moon,*
   A red medallion in the sky, a monster cameo.

*Yet somewhere, God, drenched roses bloom by fountains
   draped with mist,*
   In old, lost gardens of the earth made lyrical with rain;
*Why is it here a million brows by hungry Death are
   kissed,*
   *And here is packed, one Summer night, a whole
      world's fiery pain!*

XI

Man's greatest miracle is accomplished here.
Steeple and dome he hurls high in the air,
Until, like dreams in marble and in stone,
They lift their wonder to a world amazed.

Behind the poem is the poet's soul;

Behind the canvas throbs the artist's heart;
Behind all music lie unfanthomed tones
Known only dimly to one Master mind.
So here, when visions of new beauty rise,
Behind them float the dreams of cities old
Fallen now to silence, with the dust of kings.
Who wrought these granite ghosts, saw more than we
May ever see. He saw pale, tenuous lines
On some age-mellowed shore where cities rose
Proudly as Corinth or imperial Rome;
He saw, through mists of vision, Baghdad leap
To immaterial being, and he sought
To snatch one curve from her elusive domes;
He saw lost Nineveh and Babylon,
And Tyre, and all the golden dreams of Greece,
Columns and fanes that cannot be rebuilt,
Ev'n as Shakespearian lines can never sing
Again on any poet's resplendent page.
But the vague Source of these most lovely things
Were his for one high instant; and he caught
Their spirit and their glory for all time.
These are the shadows of far nobler walls,
The wraiths of ancient pomp and glittering days,
Set here by master minds and master souls,
Almost as wonderful as mountains are,
Mysterious as the petals of a flower.

XII

On Winter nights, when the clean snow falls down
Like white flowers from the meadows of the sky,
You hear the motors thundering on their way
To fashionable caravanseries,

The theatre or the opera, or the ball.
In bright array the shimmering women sit
Where clinking glasses make their pleasant sound,
And laughter is the gay room's only creed.
Music and lights and beauty—yes, and love—
They make good company on windy nights
When one must somehow manage to forget
The bitterness the season has brought on.
Well, mirth is found here—mirth and revelry;
Let red wine flow, and let the champagne shine
First in its goblet, then in many eyes,
Till the great room seems greater than before,
The music sweeter, women lovelier,
And Love itself, that is the best of all,
Bigger than heaven and earth rolled into one!

This is the way to kill life's youthful hours—
These are the places to erase the thought
Of poverty and penury and grief—
Here where mad, jocund conversation hums,
And masks but lure one to imagine all
The tragedy behind such flimpsy screens.
It lends an interest to Life to know
That there beside that *grand dame* proudly pale,
Sits a young courtesan whose story is
The common topic of a trivial world.
They would not dine together in *her* home,
They would not sit in the same costly box
At either Opera House; but here—well, this
Alters the case, each one would quickly say;
The harlot gives the *grand dame* something strange
To think of through this tedious dining hour,
And then—who knows?—perhaps the painted girl
Finds very much to ruminate upon

When her quick eyes consider the Lady's face!
How many a flash of understanding whirls
Across the gilded room, one may not know;
But always when I sit in such a place,
And see the comprehension in the eyes
Of men and women of divided spheres,
I think that no such distance separates
The half-world and the world as that which flings
The rich and poor immesurably apart!

When it is time to go they hurry out
To find their motors, and they mark how cold
The wind is; but they seldom toss a coin
To the poor newsboy, shivering near the door.

Out on the jewelled Avenue they see
A priest upon his way to say a prayer
Over a dying man; and for one brief,
Incalculable instant, who may guess
What thoughts are in the merry revellers' minds?
They may have craved the peace he seems to know,
The calm and quiet of his spiritual face;
And to the priest there may have come a wish,
However vague, to snatch one moment's joy
From this apparent happiness and mirth.

They pass the Bread Line—but they do not care,
Flushed now with wine, at ease with all the world;
They hear a street evangelist's faint whine,
And the Salvation Army's simple songs;
They laugh at these—they are not picturesque—
And yet, perhaps, they serve their purposes!

So speed these careless groups upon their way,

Poorer than all the mendicants they pass,
And sad in their false joy and harlotry,
Rich only in their prejudice and pride.

XIII

I said one day that I would leave the town,
Its madness and pretensions and despair,
And follow once again the ways that lead
To the large wisdom of the wilderness,
And the great mercy of the solitude.
I could not bear the city's ceaseless groans,
Her murmur as of constant weariness,
That echoed and re-echoed like the sound
Of waves upon some memory-haunted shore.
My spirit could not prosper while my heart
Was torn by her continual desire
To scourge her children with her cruel rod.

I fled from her, and looked with sorrow back
Upon this tangled tumult, wondering
Why I had ever loved so utterly
Her smoke-filled miles on miles of ugliness.
And then her awful beauty flashed on me,
As from the lordly Hudson 'neath the moon
I saw her rise in mystery and might,
And then remembered, while my eyes grew dim,
That I had always called this city Home.

XIV

There were wild gardens in the spaces where
I sped with eager feet; there were tall trees
Majestically lonely; and blue wastes
Of water, where it seemed no man had been;
There were long shadows in the afternoon,
And velvet evenings when the constant stars
Looked down on me, lost in the perfumed dark;
There were clean rains—baptismal showers that fell
Upon my brow; and mornings shot with threads
Of beauty from the red sun's flaming loom;
And here were dreams, and pauses when it seemed
The world stood still, and Time had ceased to be;
Here energy seemed madness, speech a sin,
And Life one long *Laudate* without end.

I shall not ever know how many days
Had marched away, when first I heard the Sound,
The Quiet Voice that murmured in the trees
And spoke at last so that I understood.
I only know I followed when it called,
I only know I went the way it led,
Back to the old, sweet bondage, as a man
Returns to Love, however sad Love be.

When, sick of all the sorrow and distress
  That flourished in the city like foul weeds,
  I sought blue rivers and green, opulent meads,
And leagues of unregarded loneliness
Whereon no foot of man had seemed to press,
  I did not know how great had been my needs,
  How wise the woodland's gospels and her creeds,
How good her faith to one long comfortless.

But in the silence came a Voice to me;
  In every wind it murmured, and I knew
    It would not cease, though far my heart might roam.
  It called me in the sunrise and the dew,
At noon and twilight, sadly, hungrily,
  The jealous City, whispering always—"Home!"

City Roofs
(From the Metroplitan Tower)

Roof-tops, roof-tops, what do you cover?
Sad folk, bad folk, and many a glowing lover;
Wise people, simple people, children of despair—
Roof-tops, roof-tops, hiding pain and care.

Roof-tops, roof-tops, O what sin you're knowing,
While above you in the sky the white clouds are
    blowing;
While beneath you, agony and dolor and grim strife
Fight the olden battle, the olden war of Life.

Roof-tops, roof-tops, cover up their shame—
Wretched souls, prisoned souls too piteous to name;
Man himself hath built you all to hide away the stars—
Roof-tops, roof-tops, you hide ten million scars.

Roof-tops, roof-tops, well I know you cover
Many solemn tragedies, and many a lonely lover;
But ah! you hide the good that lives in the throbbing
    city—
Patient wives, and tenderness, forgiveness, faith, and
    pity.

Roof-tops, roof-tops, this is what I wonder:
You are thick as poisonous plants, thick the people
   under;
Yet roofless, and homeless, and shelterless they roam,
The driftwood of the town who have no roof-top and
   no home!

The Prison

I went through a crowded city—
   A city within my own—
Whose houses were of iron
   And terrible grey stone.

I saw each awful doorway
   With clanging lock and key,
And faces white behind them,
   Most pitiful to me.

There was a patient silence
   Within this town of tears,
That told me more than lips could
   Of long, bleak, maddening years.

That silence—and those faces!
   They haunt me all the while;
Yet why should dead men whisper,
   And why should dead men smile?

Retreat
(For F. Walter Taylor)

I know a bookshop in a quiet street
  Close to the flame and thunder of Broadway,
A little heaven, a refuge and retreat
  From the loud murmur of the starting day.

There, in the hush, with voices of the past
  Singing far songs—Wordsworth and Keats and
    Poe—
Often I linger, dipping in the last
  Bright volume, or some ancient folio.

The world goes by; haply is lost—well lost,
  But old words rise before me in this place,
And in some shining book, by Love embossed,
  I read the record of a nobler race.

I read of pomp and chivalry and pride,
  Or the light laughter of a quiet age;
I dwell in moonlight on a distant tide,
  What time I thumb and turn some yellow page.

I hear the rustle of imperial lace,
  I dream of glory and strong, fighting men. . . .
The lamps expire, and in the chimney-place
  The last red embers burn, go out; and then

I find myself one of the evening crowd,
  Facing the world that thrills me as before.
But O that moment when they spoke aloud—
  Shakespeare and Dante—through Death's hidden
    door!

Fifth Avenue At Night

Like moonstones drooping from a fair queen's ears
   The pale lights seem—
White gems that shimmer when the dark appears
   And the old dream—

The ancient dream that comes with every night
   Through the long street—
The quiet and the shadows, and the light
   Tread of far feet.

Broadway

Here surge the ceaseless caravans,
   Here throbs the city's heart,
And down the street each takes his way
   To play his little part.

The tides of life flow on, flow on,
   And Laughter meets Despair;
A heart might break along Broadway. . . .
   I wonder who would care?

Downtown

The sun has gone, and from the ferryboat
   That like a golden worm crawls through the night,
I watch the myriad stars that round me float,
   And, cityward, the honeycombs of light.

Tier after tier, they blossom in the dark,
  Miraculously radiant, while I
Think of the toilers bent beneath each spark,
  And breathe a little prayer for them, and sigh.

New Buildings

The turrets leap higher and higher,
  And the little old homes go down;
The workmen pound on the iron and steel—
  The woodpeckers of the town.

The Lights

Ten thousand jewels flash out
  When the darkness of night appears;
But O I sometimes think these pearls
  Are ten thousand people's tears—

Ten thousand tears that are shed
  Through the terrible strife of the day,
And doomed to shine through the city's night
  Till the stars have faded away.

Traffic

Hoof-beats thundering on the paves,
  Wagons crashing by.
(But O I dream of distant waves,
  God's tent of open sky!)

Bells that clamor all day long,
  Rush and roar of steam.
(But I have heard a robin's song,
  If only in my dream!)

To a Hurdy-Gurdy
(Playing on Sixth Avenue)

Here's to you, brave Hurdy-gurdy,
  Grinding out your happy tune
While the traffic round you rumbles,
  In the city's Summer noon.

No one hears you! Yet the rapture
  That you feel, despite our faults,
As you gaily give the measure
  Of the latest merry waltz!

Trams are rolling all about you—
  How the Elevated roars!
And above their noise and tumult
  Your thin twanging vainly soars.

Good for you, poor Hurdy-gurdy!
  Play, unheard, your little part;
Would that I could sing as you do,
  With but half as brave a heart!

The Voices

I heard the voice of the city,
  Calling again and again,
And into her arms there hastened
  Millions and millions of men.

And I heard the voice of old gardens,
  Of quiet woodland ways;
But few there were who would heed them
  In the rush of the busy days.

The cities grow old and vanish,
  And their people faint and die;
But the gardens are green forever,
  Forever blue is the sky!

Next Door

We saw the tapers burn
  In the home so close to ours;
But however our hearts might yearn,
  We dared not send our flowers.
"He will not understand," we said,
"Our loving thought of his loved dead."

O City! thus you hide
  The pity in every heart!
Those who are at our side
  You sunder a world apart.
A little barrier built of stone—
And my neighbor grieves—alone, alone!

The Parks

There are green islands in the city sea,
  Where all day long, the endless, passionate waves
  Beat, yet destroy not; and their quiet saves
How many a heart grown sick with memory!

Not derelicts alone are foundered there,
  But children with the laughter of the May—
  Bright, living flowers—in these glad gardens play,
Knowing, yet knowing not, the town's despair!

God made the ocean, where tumultuously
  The loud storms burst; and Babylon He made;
  Yet all the hills are His, dim valley and glade—
There are green islands in the city sea.

A City Sunset

Across the roof-tops of the town
I saw the flaming sun go down;
For some, another day of tears
Lay buried in the hurrying years.

The shadows folded; here and there
A yellow light began to flare.
For some, another golden day
Of gladness sped upon its way.

125

Around the Corner

Around the corner I have a friend,
In this great city that has no end;
Yet the days go by, and weeks rush on,
And before I know it a year is gone,
And I never see my old friend's face,
For Life is a swift and terrible race.
He knows I like him just as well
As in the days when I rang his bell
And he rang mine. We were younger then,
And now we are busy, tired men:
Tired with playing a foolish game,
Tired of trying to make a name.
"To-morrow," I say, "I will call on Jim,
Just to show that I'm thinking of him."
But to-morrow comes—and to-morrow goes,
And distance between us grows and grows.

Around the corner!—yet miles away. . . .
"Here's a telegram, sir. . . ."
                    "Jim died to-day."
And that's what we get, and deserve in the end:
Around the corner, a vanished friend.

Herman Scheffauer

Manhattan

Atlantes of the firmament! abrupt
  The granite monsters of Manhattan frown,—
Phalanx of Titans, stark and interrupt,
  Their tyrannous grim bulks oppress the town.

Their gonfalons and vaporous plumes at play
  Stream rhythmic to the city's stormy beat,
Her giant pulse that goads the groaning day
  To pile its mortal labor at their feet.

The stunned sea clasps the aching iron isle
  That holds eternal tumult in its heart,
While Greed's great laugh from pile to towering pile,
  Leaps in relentless triumph o'er the mart.

Incessant roars her fevered race of lives
  Crushed through the sunless channels of her stone,
Or flung across the paths where Mammon drives
  His chariot wheels o'er ways of flesh and bone.

What brand upon the brow of man? what mark
  That hounds worn spirits toward a glittering goal?
Where Luxury lifts her ashen husks, and dark
Earth idols force their usury from the soul.

O thunder-wrought Manhattan! shaped of gold
  Thy tongue, thine eyes of blind basalt, of steel
Thy smothered breasts still young—yet bleak and old
  The mountainous gray weariness they feel.

Thy life is eaten by thine eagerness,
   And round thy doomward sandals whirlwinds roar,
And round thy wreck-mad walls the tempest's stress
   Riots from adamantine shore to shore.

Now Anarchs of Annihilation take
   Their sleep of golden torpor in the glow
Of thy sky-storming summits—when they wake
   What ruin red shall their war-trumpets blow?

"An Amiable Child"
(On its Grave near Grant's Tomb, New York)

Dust of a bud of Spring,
   Dust of a long-dead child,
How deep in saintly slumber!
   Though myriad footsteps ring
     On paves by crime defiled,
Where woes of men encumber
   These grasses wet and wild.

Calm be thy sleep beside
   The river visions fair,
Unstirred by that dark river
   Of Life whose downward tide
     Bears wreckage of Despair,
Where lips, like wounds that quiver,
   Move bloody with a prayer.

Oft silent pass the hosts
   By fever-phantoms led,
Where glooms the murky city,—

Silent to thee as ghosts
    That mourn young flowers fled;
Their steps weave spells of pity
    And memory o'er thy head.

    High o'er the morselled stone
        The hero's pyramid
In haggard granite towers
    Enormous, bleak and lone,
        But where thy curls lie hid,
Fall sun and rain and showers
    Warm from the full eyelid.

    Thy grave seems like a song
        Of peace in iron frays,
A voice o'er wastes of madness,
    Greed, misery and wrong,
        A voice that might upraise
Thy bright and infant gladness
    To bless our loveless days.

    O storm-shod centuries!
        Here grow your sick souls well,
Where this dead child is lying
    'Neath olden stones and trees,
        Where one sweet word shall tell
Of a tenderness undying
    And the heart where it did dwell.

Thomas Augustine Daly

Een Napoli

Here een Noo Yorka, where am I
　　Seence I am landa las' July,
All gray an' ogly ees da sky,
　　An' cold as eet can be.
But steell so long I maka mon',
So long ees worka to be done,
I can forget how shines da sun
　　Een Napoli.

But oh, w'en pass da boy dat sal
Da violets, an' I can smal
How sweet dey are, I no can tal
　　How seeck my heart ees be.
I no can work, how mooch I try,
But only seet an' wondra why
I could not justa leeve an' die
　　Een Napoli.

Charles Coleman Stoddard

When Broadway Was A Country Road

No rushing cars, nor tramping feet
    Disturbed the peaceful summer days
That shone as now upon the street
    That knows our busy, noisy ways.
    And blushing girls and awkward jays
Strolled slowly home, and cattle lowed
    As fell the purple twilight haze,
When Broadway was a country road.

No tailored dandies, trim and neat;
    No damsels of the latest craze
Of form and fashion; no conceit
    To catch the fancy or amaze.
    No buildings met the skyward gaze;
Nor myriad lights that nightly glowed
    To set the midnight hour ablaze—
When Broadway was a country road.

Then shady lanes with blossoms sweet
    Led gently down to quiet bays
Or to the sheltered, hedged retreat
    Some falling mansion now betrays.
    The stage-coach here no longer pays
Its daily call, nor farmers goad
    Their oxen, as in olden days
When Broadway was a country road.

Little indeed to meet the praise
Of modern times the picture showed.
　　And yet the fancy fondly strays
To Broadway as a country road.

Louise Morgan Smith Sill

Bowling Green, New York

Where the city's rushing throng
Beats its burly way along
    Whitehall Street,
Up where giant buildings frown
On the pygmy people, down
    At their feet,

Lies a modest bit of park
That the people seldom mark
    In their haste,
As they scatter to and fro,
And like winds of heaven go,
    Fury-paced.

But within this green enclosed,—
Where the burghers, once reposed
    At their ease,
Or at bowls displayed their skill
Summer afternoons to kill,
    If you please—

Reigns some magic of the past
That, amid the noisy blast
    All around,
Sets a charm upon your ear
As you enter, and you hear
    Not a sound;

Not a murmur, save the tone

Of a Dutchman, or the drone
    Of a bee;
Or the laughter of a child
As he scampers free and wild
    On the lea.

You can see the Maying-time,
When the maiden's voices chime
    Joyous notes;
When the Neltjes and the rest
Are arrayed in all their best
    Petticoats.

And they dance with such a grace,
And they blush with such a face—
    Rose-and-cream—
As they curtsey, sweet and shy,
That you wonder why you sigh
    As you dream.

For they've vanished long ago,
Burgher, goede vrouw and beau,
    Damsel fair;
And the smile that meets your eye,
And the steps that patter by
    Are but air.

Yet, 'tis said that every night
When the moon is shining bright
    On the scene,
Still the Dutchmen's placid souls
Play their solemn game of bowls
    On the Green.

Maiden Lane, New York

Down Maiden Lane, where clover grew,
  Sweet-scented in the early air,
Where sparkling rills went shining through
  Their grassy banks, so green, so fair,
Blithe little maids from Holland land
  Went tripping, laughing each to each,
To bathe the flax, or spread a band
  Of linen in the sun to bleach.

More than two centuries ago
  They wore this path—a maiden's lane—
Where now such waves of commerce flow
  As never dazed a burgher's brain.
Two hundred years ago and more
  Those thrifty damsels, one by one,
With plump, round arms their linen bore
  To dry in Mana-ha-ta's sun.

But now! Behold the altered view;
  No tender sward, no bubbling stream,
No laughter,—was it really true,
  Or but the fancy of a dream?
Were these harsh walls a byway sweet,
  This floor of stone a grassy plain?
Pray vanish, modern city street,
  And let us stroll down Maiden Lane!

Marianne Moore

Dock Rats

There are human beings who seem to regard the place
  as craftily as we do—who seem to feel that it is a
  good place to come home to. On what a river;
  wide—twinkling like a chopped sea under some
    of the finest shipping in the

world: the square-rigged four-master, the liner, the
  battleship like the two-thirds submerged section of
  an iceberg; the tug—strong-moving thing, dip-
  ping and pushing, the bell striking as it comes; the
    steam yacht, lying like a new made arrow on the

stream; the ferry-boat—a head assigned, one to
  each compartment, making a row of chessmen set
  for play. When the wind is from the east, the
  smell is of apples; of hay, the aroma increased and
    decreased suddenly as the wind changes;

of rope; of mountain leaves for florists. When it is
  from the west, it is an elixir. There is oc
  casionally a parokeet
  arrived from Brazil, clasping and clawing; or a
    monkey—tail and feet in readiness for an over-

ture. All palms and tail; how delightful! There is
  the sea, moving the bulkhead with its horse
  strength; and the multiplicity of rudders and pro-
  pellors; the signals, shrill, questioning, per-

emptory, diverse; the wharf cats and the barge
dogs—it

is easy to overestimate the value of such things.
One does not live in such a place from motives of
expediency but because to one who has been ac-
customed to it, shipping is the most congenial
thing in the world.

Siegfried Sassoon

Storm on Fifth Ave

A sallow waiter brings me six huge oysters . . .
Gloom shutters up the sunset with a plague
Of unpropitious twilight jagged asunder
By flashlight demonstrations. *Gee, what a peach
Of a climate!* (Pardon slang: these sultry storms
Afflict me with neurosis: rumbling thunder
Shakes my belief in academic forms.)

An oyster-coloured atmospheric rumpus
Beats up to blot the sunken daylight's gildings.
Against the looming cloud-bank, ivory-pale,
Stand twenty-storied blocks of office-buildings.
Snatched upward on a gust, lost news-sheets sail
Waif-like in lone areas of mid-air;
Flapping like melancholy kites, they scare
My gaze, a note of wildness in the scene.

Out on the pattering side-walk, people hurry
For shelter, while the tempest swoops to scurry
Across to Brooklyn. Bellying figures clutch
At wide-brimmed hats and bend to meet the weather,
Alarmed for fresh-worn silks and flurried feather.

Then hissing deluge splashes down to beat
The darkly glistening flatness of the street.
Only the cars nose on through rain-lashed twilight:
Only the Sherman Statue, angel-guided,
Maintains its mock-heroic martial gesture.

A sallow waiter brings me beans and pork.
Outside there's fury in the firmament.
Ice-cream, of course, will follow; and I'm content. . . .
O Babylon! O Carthage! O New York!

Midnight on Broadway

Under the cold brown canopy of heaven
Huge winking signs, unflickering gold facades,
Relentlessly proclaim the cheap-jack fame
Of Movie Stars, and Chewing Gum, and Tires.

The heaped snow has an artificial look
As if impersonating sifted sugar,
Along the melting sidewalks, blurred and trodden,
It clogs the feet of jostling crowds that shuffle
Through Broadway shlush with faces greenish-pale
Each face in spot-light of magnesium noon.

The doors of Drama swallow and disgorge them
In soda-bars they sup: to-night's the night!
And Time, dissolved from frozen floating lumps
To multicolored spoonfuls of ice-cream,
Fades on the incandescence of their breath,
Whose jazz of glory is a dance of death.

But *Wrigley's Gum*, flanked by cascading peacocks.
Mints the one dream, "to chew or not to chew."
If that's the question, you can solve it quick:
Ten cents and your saliva do the trick!

Edwin Curran

Manhattan

Oh, marble-spired Manhattan, I look into your
thousand eyes at dusk,
And your thousand eyes look back at me, kindled
with lights over the harbor.

You hold the sky set like blue wings on your mountain
peaks of splendor,
And you will hold the sky until the world ends and
the dream is gone, Oh Manhattan.

Toss your towers into the stars, Great Gray City!
Lift your peaks until they push over the clouds;
Live and throb and beat your mighty heart against
the solid sun;
You are eternal, Great White City!

Walk over your bridges of the centuries, Oh Manhattan,
glorious Manhattan;
Tread upon the aeons of your remarkable destiny of
the future,
Imperishable, perpetual, everlasting Manhattan!

I look into your thousand eyes, and your thousand
eyes look into my eyes.
I look into your face, and your face is full of the
glory of God.
I look into your soul, and your soul is full of the
wonder of the world;
Oh nourishing, immortal, beautiful Manhattan.

Nothing is so eternalas a city, and you are the eternal
     city of eternal cities,
Pavemented, walled, carred, lighted, jeweled, crowded
     city of beauty,
God's own city of the western world.

Your ferry boats walk the salt wave crowded;
Your tugs are the organs of the harbor singing their
     deep and sonorous hymns of commerce;
Your walls, New York, hold up heaven, parapets of
     beauty stabbing into the stars!
Pillars of the universe.

Oh music in stone, poetry in sculpture, song in
     architectual marble, prayer in granite, an ecstasy
     in steel and iron and gold, singing city of the
     great heart, singing city,
You are Manhattan!

Anna Hempstead Branch

Sonnets For New York City

I
New York At Sunrise

When with her clouds the early dawn illumes
Our doubtful streets, wistful they grow and mild;
As if a sleeping soul grew happy and smiled,
The whole dark city radiantly blooms.
Pale spires lift their hands above the glooms
Like a resurrection, delicately wild,
And flushed with slumber like a little child,
Under a mist, shines forth the innocent Tombs.
Thus have I seen it from a casement high.
As unsubstantial as a dream it grows.
Is this Manhattan, virginal and shy,
That in a cloud so rapturously glows?
Ethereal, frail, and like an opening rose,
I see my city with an enlightened eye.

II
A Political "Boss"

Has he no country? Is he of alien breed?
Is this land not his home? Oh, exiled one!
Stranger to his own kind, where does he run?
How he has shamed us, for the world to read!
Oh, carrion, prowling where this people bleed,
Grown fat upon disaster, hide from the sun!
A scornful nation asks, what has he done

With the public trust, the honor, and the need.
Not him with glorious hand will we indite,
Patriot, Statesman, in the Hall of Fame,
Nor will we let him flee into the night
Of safe oblivion! But oh—that name
For our sons' sons a moving hand shall write
In scarlet letters on the walls of Shame.

III
Shame on thee, O Manhattan

Shame on thee, O Manhattan, whom I love!
And shame on me that I have slept away
So many years while thy feet went astray!
O Thou—that should'st be white as any dove,
Thou Scarlet Woman! Is there no voice to move—
No hand to smite us? Even for this I pray—
Some terrible scourging that we have let the day
Darken around us while we saw thee rove.
Last night I heard thee cry. Thy wandering feet
Went bleeding by me. On thy ruined breast
I saw thee nurse a feeding child of flame!
Desolate, gorgeous, frantic along the street!
Ah, how I blushed in the dark that through my rest
I felt the burning garments of thy shame.

IV
The Fountain of Life

This day into the fields my steps are led.
I cannot heal me there! Row after row,
Thousands of daisies radiantly blow.

They have not brought from Heaven my daily bread!
But they are like a prayer too often said.
I have forgot their meaning, and I go
From the cold rubric of their gold and snow,
And the calm ritual, all uncomforted.
I want the faces! faces! remote and pale,
That surge along the city streets! The flood
Of reckless ones, haggard and spent and frail,
Excited, hungry! In this other mood
'T is not the words of the faith for which I ail,
But to plunge in the fountain of its living blood.

To a New York Shop-Girl Dressed For Sunday

To-day I saw the shop-girl go
Down gay Broadway to meet her beau.

Conspicuous, splendid, conscious, sweet,
She spread abroad and took the street.

And all that niceness would forbid,
Superb, she smiled upon and did.

Let other girls, whose happier days
Preserve the perfume of their ways,

Go modestly. The passing hour
Adds splendor to their opening flower.

But from this child too swift a doom
Must steal her prettiness and bloom,

Toil and weariness hide the grace
That pleads a moment from her face.

So blame her not if for a day
She flaunts her glories while she may.

She half perceives, half understands,
Snatching her gifts with both her hands.

The little strut beneath the skirt
That lags neglected in the dirt,

The indolent swagger down the street—
Who can condemn such happy feet!

Innocent! vulgar—that's the truth!
Yet with the darling wiles of youth!

The bright, self-conscious eyes that stare
With such hauteur, beneath such hair!
Perhaps the men will find me fair!

Charming and charmed, flippant, arrayed,
Fluttered and foolish, proud, displayed,
Infinite pathos of parade!

The bangles and the narrowed waist—
The tinseled boa—forgive the taste!
Oh, the starved nights she gave for that,
And bartered bread to buy her hat!

She flows before the reproachful sage
And begs her woman's heritage.

Dear child, with the defiant eyes,
Insolent with the half surmise
We do not quite admire, I know
How foresight frowns on this vain show!

And judgment, wearily sad, may see
No grace in such frivolity.

Yet which of us was ever bold
To worship Beauty, hungry and cold!

Scorn famine down, proudly expressed
Apostle to what things are best.

Let him who starves to buy the food
For his soul's comfort find her good,

Nor chide the frills and furbelows
That are the prettiest things she knows.

Poet and prophet in God's eyes
Make no more perfect sacrifice.

Who knows before what inner shrine
She eats with them the bread and wine?

Poor waif! One of the sacred few
That madly sought the best they knew!

Dear—let me lean my cheek to-night
Close, close to yours. Ah, that is right.

How warm and near! At last I see
One beauty shines for thee and me.

So let us love and understand—
Whose hearts are hidden in God's hand.

And we will cherish your brief Spring
And all its fragile flowering.

God loves all prettiness, and on this
Surely his angels lay their kiss.

Timeline

1900: Ellis Island reopens after renovations.

1902: A train service between Chicago and New York begins.

1902: Kosher beef prices in America jump from 12 cents to 18 cents a pound causing riots.

1903: The New York Stock Exchange opens it's first building at 10 Broad St.

1904: A fire aboard a steamboat on the East River kills 1,021 people.

1904: The Jewish Museum of New York City is founded.

1905: The first gasoline-powered buses in America begin running along Fifth Avenue.

1908: New York Taxi Cab Company runs 700 taxis on the streets of New York.

1909: The National Association for the Advancement of Colored People is founded.

1909: The Queensboro Bridge over the East River is completed.

1909: The first subway car with side doors goes into service.

1909: The Metropolitan Tower is completed.

1911: The Triangle Shirtwaist Factory Fire kills 146 workers.

1912: The Jewish volunteer women's organization, Hadassah, is founded.

1913: After renovations, the new Grand Central Terminal is open.

1913: The Woolworth Building is completed.

1914: World War I begins.

1915: Over 25,000 women march up Fifth Avenue advocating for women's suffrage.

1917: New York grants women the right to vote.

1918: Lola Ridge's *The Ghetto, and Other Poems* is published.

1920: Evelyn Scott's *Precipitations* is published.

1921: The New York Transit Comission tries to solve overcrowding and delays on the sub way.

1922: The New York Stock Exchange expands by adding a building on 11 Broad Street for new offices and a new trading floor.

1923: Maxwell Bodenheim's *Against this Age* is published.

Suggested Reading

Bodenheim, Maxwell. *Against this Age*. Bondi and Liveright, 1923.

Burnet, Dana. *Poems*. Harper & Brothers, 1915.

LaFemina, Gerry, editor. *Token Entry: New York City Subway Poems*. Smalls Books, 2012.

McKay, Claude. *Harlem Shadows: the Poems of Claude Mckay*. Harcourt, Brace, 1922.

Oppenheim, James. *Monday Morning: And Other Poems*. Sturgis & Walton Company, 1909.

Reznikoff, Charles. *The Poems of Charles Reznikoff: 1918-1975*. Edited by Seamus Cooney, Black Sparrow Press, 2005.

Schmidt, Elizabeth, editor. *Poems of New York*. A.A. Knopf, 2002.

Scott, Evelyn. *Precipitations*. Nicholas L. Brown, 1920.

Teasdale, Sara. *Rivers to the Sea*. Macmillan Company, 1915.

Toorawa, Shawkat M, editor. *The City That Never Sleeps: Poems of New York*. State University of New York Press, 2015.

Towne, Charles Hanson. *The Quiet Singer: And Other Poems*. Mitchell Kennerley, 1914.

VanDyke, Henry. *The Poems of Henry VanDyke*. Charles
   Scriber's Sons, 1920.

Williams, William Carlos. *Sour Grapes: A Book of Poems*.
   The Four Seas Company, 1921.

Wolf, Stephen, editor. *I Speak of the City: Poems of New
   York*. Columbia University Press, 2007.